PRAISE FOR *GOD IN SLOW MOTION*

"Italians sometimes say that a good book is 'read in one breath.' *God in Slow Motion* is just such a book. It whizzes and bursts like a firework, but there is deep biblical grounding, wide cultural engagement, and lasting aftershocks that open up crevices to truth you never knew existed. You're one breath away from transformation."

—LEONARD SWEET, BEST-SELLING AUTHOR, PROFESSOR (DREW UNIVERSITY, GEORGE FOX UNIVERSITY), AND CHIEF CONTRIBUTOR TO SERMONS.COM

"'We divert our attention from Christ's loving, redemptive intent and focus our eyes only on our own feeble attempts at man-made redemption.' Insight like this is what makes *God in Slow Motion* a great read. Like cool water in a hot desert, it refreshes any of us who may have grown too casual to the all-consuming love of a glorious Savior."

—BILL MYERS, FILM PRODUCER AND BEST-SELLING AUTHOR (*THE GOD HATER: ELI*)

"With characteristic eloquence, *God in Slow Motion* wanders through vignettes from the life of Jesus, looking for the glory that hides beneath the surface of the Gospel stories. In the process, Mike Nappa provides a beautifully fresh perspective on truths about grace and glory that may have grown too familiar."

—TIMOTHY PAUL JONES, PHD, ASSOCIATE VICE PRESIDENT FOR ONLINE EDUCATION AT THE SOUTHERN BAPTIST THEOLOGICAL SEMINARY

"In *God in Slow Motion*, Mike Nappa gently lifts God's truths from the pages of Scripture, giving us a peek at glory und— ds of Life. Powerful, poignant stories to cross, through mysteries and grace, ings with wonder to the life-giving, m nd your-self (and your faith) reaching o page."

—TIM WESEMANN, BEST-SEL ...ᴏʀ ʙAUER'S HAVING A BAD DAY

"With elegant simplicity, Mike Nappa brings to life key biblical passages and core aspects of the Christian faith in a manner that feels like a wonder-filled campfire chat. Nappa injects life, mystery, and curiosity into a faith that for many has become stale. *God in Slow Motion* is that rare Christian book I'd feel comfortable handing a nonbelieving friend. It makes the case for Christianity not by way of facts or formulas, nor by claiming that faith in Christ is about 'your best life now!' self-help. It simply focuses on Jesus, that 'man of sorrows' who invites us to follow him even through our pain, suffering, questions, and doubts."

—BRETT MCCRACKEN, MANAGING EDITOR OF *BIOLA MAGAZINE* AND POPULAR AUTHOR OF *HIPSTER CHRISTIANITY*

GOD IN
SLOW
MOTION

GOD IN SLOW MOTION

REFLECTIONS ON JESUS AND THE 10 UNEXPECTED
LESSONS YOU CAN SEE IN HIS LIFE

MIKE NAPPA

THOMAS NELSON
Since 1798

NASHVILLE   DALLAS   MEXICO CITY   RIO DE JANEIRO

Published in Nashville, Tennessee, by Thomas Nelson. Thomas Nelson is a registered trademark of Thomas Nelson, Inc.

Thomas Nelson, Inc., titles may be purchased in bulk for educational, business, fundraising, or sales promotional use. For information, please e-mail SpecialMarkets@ThomasNelson.com.

God in Slow Motion is published in association with Nappaland Literary Agency, an independent agency dedicated to publishing works that are: Authentic. Relevant. Eternal. Visit us on the web at: NappalandLiterary.com

To protect the privacy of those who have shared their stories with the author, some details and names have been changed. Additionally, quoted conversations involving the author, while true to the intent, have been recreated from the author's memory and may not be word-for-word.

Unless otherwise marked, Scripture quotations are from the Holy Bible, New International Version®, NIV®. Copyright © 1973, 1978, 1984, 2011 by Biblica, Inc.™ Used by permission of Zondervan. All rights reserved worldwide. www.zondervan.com

Scripture quotations marked NLT are from the *Holy Bible*, New Living Translation. © 1996. Used by permission of Tyndale House Publishers, Inc., Wheaton, Illinois 60189. All rights reserved.

Scripture quotations marked NKJV are from THE NEW KING JAMES VERSION. © 1982 by Thomas Nelson, Inc. Used by permission. All rights reserved.

Scripture quotations marked NASB are from the NEW AMERICAN STANDARD BIBLE®, © The Lockman Foundation 1960, 1962, 1963, 1968, 1971, 1972, 1973, 1975, 1977, 1995. Used by permission.

Scripture quotations marked ESV are from THE ENGLISH STANDARD VERSION. © 2001 by Crossway Bibles, a division of Good News Publishers.

Scripture quotations marked HCSB are from the HOLMAN CHRISTIAN STANDARD BIBLE. © 1999, 2000, 2002, 2003 by Broadman and Holman Publishers. All rights reserved.

Scripture quotations marked NCV are from the New Century Version®. © 2005 by Thomas Nelson, Inc. Used by permission. All rights reserved.

Scripture quotations marked KJV are from the King James Version.

Portions of chapter 2, "Mysterious Grace," are adapted and reprinted from *Thirsty* by Amy Nappa, © 2008 Nappaland Communications, Inc. All rights reserved. Adapted and reprinted by permission. Portions of chapter 3, "Criminal Kindness," are adapted and reprinted from *Tuesdays with Matthew* by Mike Nappa, © 2003 Nappaland Communications, Inc. All rights reserved. Adapted and reprinted by permission.

While the author has made every effort to provide accurate telephone numbers, Internet addresses, and other contact information at the time of publication, neither the publisher nor the author assumes any responsibility for errors, or for changes that occur after publication. Further, the publisher does not have any control over and does not assume any responsibility for author or third-party websites or their content.

The publisher assumes no responsibility for any factual errors that may stem from the use of Wikipedia.com as a source for some material in this book.

Library of Congress Cataloging-in-Publication Data

Nappa, Mike, 1963-
  God in slow motion : reflections on Jesus and the 10 unexpected lessons you can see in his life / Mike Nappa.
    pages cm
  Includes bibliographical references.
  ISBN 978-1-4002-0462-5
  1. Jesus Christ. I. Title.
  BT304.N37 2013
  232.9'04--dc23   2012048763

Printed in the United States of America
13 14 15 16 17 RRD 5 4 3 2 1

For Anthony Evangel, who inspires
me to look for God.

God chose the foolish things of the world to shame the wise;
God chose the weak things of the world to shame the strong.

—THE APOSTLE PAUL, 1 CORINTHIANS 1:27

CONTENTS

CONTENTS

THE RACEHORSE

H ere are the names that matter for this story:
Eadweard.
Leland.
And, of course, Occident.

There's also the issue of $25,000, the amount of the alleged wager that was the catalyst for this whole grand enterprise. But that part we'll talk about later. For now, let's simply focus on Eadweard, Leland, Occident, and the history about to be made.

The adventure began with a horse. And a racetrack. And people possessing more money than sense.

It was spring of 1872 at the vast California estate of one Leland Stanford—former governor of California and president of Central Pacific Railroad. The American dream had been good to Governor Stanford, making him a millionaire several times over. In return, Leland gave two things back to posterity: one is the prestigious place of learning that still bears his name, Stanford University. The other was a gentleman's wager about a horse.

Those who tell the stories say Leland Stanford put up a whopping $25,000 for his side of the bet. Others dismiss that as mere hearsay, deriding the idea that this "sanctimonious" railway baron would degenerate into something as lewd and lowbred as gambling. Regardless of whether or not a formal wager actually existed, the fact is that Governor Stanford did put up his own money to settle the bet.

Which was, as we've indicated, about a horse. Or more specifically, about what happens *underneath* a racehorse, down there where hooves speed 'cross the dusty ground, caught up in motion so fast their details elude even the most careful examination of the human eye.

The question itself had become known in Stanford's time as one of "unsupported transit," that is, the idea that a horse's hooves while trotting must, periodically, lose all contact with the ground. The unsupported horse, as the theory went, then continued its transit slightly airborne until the hooves touched down and repeated their stride.

Leland Stanford and his West Coast cronies subscribed fervently to the opinion that trotting racers employed unsupported transit. At the other end of the railroad tracks, on the East Coast of America, learned horsemen scoffed at that cockamamie theory. They were certain, as only experts can be, that a trotting horse always kept at least one hoof touching the ground, even at top speed. Both sides had passionate proponents and riveting arguments in defense of their respective views, but the truth was that no one could be absolutely sure. The horse's pumping hooves moved so fast that the naked eye simply couldn't see them.

That's where Eadweard came in.

In 1872, Governor Stanford decided it was time to settle, once and for all, the debate over unsupported transit. To that end, he hired noted photographer Eadweard Muybridge to take high-speed photographs of his thoroughbred racehorse, Occident, in full trot around the track on Stanford's California estate. The only problem was that no camera apparatus had yet been invented that could capture the blurred motion of Occident's speed with any kind of clarity.

It was up to Muybridge, then, to figure out how to solve that problem and, in turn, answer the burning question: Do a horse's hooves ever completely leave the ground while running?

Eadweard's innovative solution was to set up a battery of cameras alongside the racetrack and work out a system where each camera was triggered by the horse passing by. In this way he could capture, in successive frames, the continuous motion of a galloping steed. His first attempt to photograph Occident failed, but it revealed enough promise for him to reset and try again.

In May 1872, Eadweard Muybridge finally made history, catching Occident at full trot, running through twelve successive photographic images and finally settling the horsemen's debate: yes, all four of a horse's hooves do indeed leave the ground simultaneously at a regular interval within the animal's stride.

If this were any other story, that might be the end of it. But there's much more to this tale than simply *seeing* what happens underneath a racehorse; what really mattered was that someone took the time to *look*.

You see, Eadweard Muybridge's great accomplishment wasn't simply that he settled a bet. Rather, in settling that bet, he became the first to succeed at creating a usable technology for high-speed photography. His innovation thus enabled humanity to record faster-than-motion images—to see those things that happen faster than the human eye can track. The application of that new technology would, literally, change the ways of the world.

After bringing fast-motion photography into reality, Muybridge, of necessity, turned his attention to fast-motion display. He now had reliable split-second frames that could be put together to re-create on film the movement that had happened in real life. With some experimentation, Eadweard discovered that when he projected his series of photographs of Occident one after the other at rapid speed, the images blended together to give the impression of continuous motion, of "moving pictures."[1]

And that, dear friends, is how your movies began.[2]

It's hard to underestimate the impact the motion-picture industry has had on America and the world since its inception on Leland Stanford's sprawling estate. One thing is certain, though: if Eadweard Muybridge had not determined to look underneath that horse, our modern human experience would be a vastly different enterprise.

Which makes me wonder . . .

What am I missing when I speed through this life, pounding the track and letting my attention be drawn away from what's happening (figuratively) underneath my feet, just out of sight from my soul's myopic vision? What am I missing when I breeze through the gospel and gloss through pictures of the Christian life in the life of Christ? Is it merely trivia, akin to an answer to Leland's horse-racing question? Or is there something bigger, something I can't even imagine right now, waiting to be born if I simply determined to look?

That's what this book is about: the determination to *look*, to slow down the images in the gospel accounts. To see what discoveries God has for me when I look for him deep in the underneath things of Christ's life and my own.

To risk studying God . . . in slow motion.

ONE

MISCHIEVOUS GLORY

*A few minutes' walk west of Piazza del Campo, Siena's Duomo
is beyond question one of the finest Gothic cathedrals in Italy.*

—FODOR'S ITALY[1]

*He is the Messiah, the Lord . . . a baby wrapped
in cloths and lying in a manger.*

—LUKE 2:11–12

Today it seems almost a sin to walk upon the floor of the Duomo di Siena in the Tuscan region of Italy.

This is not because the *pavimentazione* (flooring) of this majestic, gothic cathedral in the historic village of Siena is necessarily holy ground. Rather it's because it feels almost immoral to smudge the print of a sneaker, a boot, or even a sandal onto the centuries-old, medieval marble masterpieces created by Domenico Beccafumi and others and inlaid into the floor of this architectural work of art.

Still, perhaps it's better to begin this story a few centuries before our time, back on an almost-forgotten day somewhere between the years 1490 and 1500, when Signore Beccafumi was yet a young boy and still unaware of the future greatness that awaited him.

If the legends are to be believed, Domenico di Pace Beccafumi was a quick-witted child with exceptional artistic talent and a fondness for practical jokes. One day Domenico's master, Mechero, sent him to buy fish from the market. Upon returning, the child gathered his painting supplies and brought them to the stone steps that rose from the street entrance of his home to the kitchen above. Then, with careful delight, he painted glistening, rainbow-colored portraits of the fish onto each of the steps in his home.

When Mechero returned a few hours later, the master looked inside and saw a cascade of his dinner strewn across the dirty steps!

Mechero's anger was immediate and fierce. He berated the boy for his carelessness and then reached down to scoop up a fish on the first stair. Only then did he discover that the fish had been painted with such care and realism that even the master artist hadn't recognized they were fake![2]

Looking back now, Domenico's little practical joke appears to have been a boy's preparation for the man's life. You see, it was only a few decades later, roughly from 1517 to 1544, when Beccafumi became the lead artist who directed the creation of the bulk of the now-legendary marble mosaic masterpieces that spread from wall to wall across the floor of the Siena Cathedral.

The Duomo di Siena features artistic flourishes all the way up to the top of its golden dome, but it's the floor that commands the greatest attention. Stretching underfoot, from edge to edge, is an intricate, ornate presentation of Bible stories told in cuts and colors of mosaic marble artwork. There are fifty-six scenes in all represented here, each painstakingly created by artists sculpting pieces of colored marble and then placing them, piece by piece, in splashes of expression within the floor. More than forty artists collectively spent almost two hundred years to complete the walkways of Siena's *duomo*.[3]

No doubt, the most influential hand of all the artists who touched this monument belonged to Domenico Beccafumi—the mischievous boy who once painted fish on steps to fool his master. Beccafumi dedicated the bulk of his adult life—almost thirty years—to crafting art for the floor of the Siena Cathedral.[4]

Looking on these now-classic visions in the marble flooring of the Duomo di Siena, one has to wonder what kind of man it would take to commit his life to sculpt excellence into the intricate details of an artistic masterpiece such as this, knowing all the while that multitudes of unwashed masses would simply trudge across his art on their way to other parts of the cathedral.

It seems a bit subversive, as if Beccafumi were daring the world to tell him that something trampled underfoot was not, and would never be, art or beauty or an image of the breathtaking glory of God.

I like that.

I like that Domenico di Pace Beccafumi, with his great talent and artistry, looked down in order to see up. I like that he dedicated his entire adult existence—the mundane moments and grandiose hours—to a project he knew would never be completed in his lifetime. That the master artist behind the glories of Siena's cathedral was once just a playful little boy with a grin on his face and a trick up his sleeve. It feels somehow elegant that this mischievous child could grow up to create works of glory that would be trampled underfoot for centuries, yet revered for all time.

It seems, well, mischievous. And glorious.

Today, as I look at Beccafumi's life's work, I suspect he must have understood something that I still have trouble getting through my thick skull: God is active in the underneath things.

Yes, there is glory in a relationship with God, and grace and joy, and much, much more. But God's glory, like the magnificence of the Duomo di Siena, most often lies humbly underfoot. It deliberately defies the definitions of our societies and our governments. It exists both in harmony with, and in antagonism toward, the values and rewards our world insists are important.

How subversive of God. It's almost as if he expects us to be in this world . . . but not of it. As if we are secret agents he intends to use to bring his glory within easy reach of the dirty, dusty, muddy people who crawl upon this earth of his.

After all, that's exactly what he did.

Unto Us a Child Is Born

They say there is no beauty without pain, no glory without sorrow. That seems to be true, even among—*especially* among—those of us whose lives are drawn toward eternity. And that's where my breath catches in my throat, where flashes of glory begin to spin in my vision:

A woman, dusty and worn from travel. A man, knowing the child his fiancée carries is not his own. Tired. Back bent. Head bowed.

A makeshift hotel room; really nothing more than a filthy animal pen. A manger; a wooden box caked with the dried saliva and leftover feed for beasts of burden.

Horror at the thought of giving birth alone, away from family, away from friends, away from home. In this awful place.

Peace from knowing that despite everything, everything will turn out right.

A God-man who propels himself willingly into the icy grip of a sin-wintered world that will only view him with mocking derision and hateful distrust. A baby, bloody and wrinkled, thrust shockingly into the world. Here, in a barn.

God, bloody and wrinkled, stowed humbly, gloriously, in the animal's food trough.[5]

And in that moment, everything changes.

Everything.

It's strange to picture in the mind's eye that moment in history when Christ was born. It feels almost wrong, unfathomable.

He who held all creation in his hand looked upon his world—and entered it from the inside. He who was Creator made himself the created. Breathed not just a slice of soul, but all of his essence into the union of a tiny egg and microscopic sperm. Planted himself deep within the woman, into the realm of time, and subject to the duress of human frailty. Nine months later he who always existed was born.

"Unto us a child is born," promised the prophet Isaiah, "unto us a son is given . . . The mighty God, The everlasting Father, The Prince of Peace" (Isaiah 9:6 KJV).

Centuries later, the physician Luke reported the fulfillment of that promise: "She [Mary] gave birth to her firstborn son," he wrote, "and she wrapped Him in cloths, and laid Him in a manger, because there was no room for them in the inn" (Luke 2:7 NASB). And then the voice of angels rang out: "Today . . . there has been born for you a Savior, who is Christ the Lord" (Luke 2:11 NASB).

God had now become also a man. Or more specifically, a helpless, vulnerable, reliably incontinent infant. He who was self-existent and in need of nothing now needed a mother's breast to feed him, her loving hand to clean away his bodily waste, her patient wisdom to teach him how to speak and walk and live.

Unfathomable.

And humiliating, especially for one such as him.

One has to ask why. This is not to question the motive of God but the method. After all, this was God incarnate, the longed-for Messiah promised to the Jewish people. The eternal King of kings! That he would be born at all was an affront; that he would be born in a rented barn was simply degrading.

So why would God choose—willingly and eagerly—to do that?

God's Reputation

My sneaking suspicion is that God's not too worried about living up to my expectations of him. Or yours. Or anyone's. His reputation in my eyes is irrelevant; his purpose in his own eyes is all that matters.

That's frustrating for me, and it's a stumbling block for many. But it's telling to look back in history and realize that Jesus fulfills every promise regarding the Messiah, yet he looks almost nothing like the expectations of the people who longed for, hoped for, and waited for his appearing.

The Jewish Messiah was (and still is) expected to come as a conquering king who would set up the rule of God upon earth, bringing peace and judgment at last. During Mary and Joseph's time, many in Israel expected their conquering Messiah to come with overwhelming suddenness and force—to bypass completely that messy, inconvenient birth-growth-boy-to-man phase. In their view, he would descend from the heavens fully formed, in miraculous power, and immediately accomplish his purpose in our world. As theologian Herschel Hobbs explains it, they envisioned "the Messiah as suddenly coming to his temple, perhaps floating down from its pinnacle amid the acclaim of the multitudes."[6]

That type of grand, glorious entrance makes sense, at least to me. After all, Jesus is the great King. He's the Alpha and Omega, the beginning and the end. He, of all people, is most deserving of accolades and overwhelming extravagance. If the King of kings is coming, then all humanity should trot out its finest, its best, its all, to welcome him. In fact, God should *demand* that of us. To do anything less would be an insult in the face of eternity, right?

And yet, that's not what God demanded. Truth is, God went out of his way to avoid doing that, choosing instead to incarnate himself in a helpless baby's body, in the second-rate city of Bethlehem. "You would think God would choose someplace elegant and grand," sings gospel music legend Andraé Crouch.[7] But God didn't do that. He deliberately chose a little, podunk, nowhere-town to be the birthplace of his finest glory. And in that small place, the greatest King ever to exist took his first human breath in a stable, with the smell of animal excrement filling the air around him.

How humiliating. How embarrassing. And how glorious.

How mischievously glorious!

God, in his great wisdom, thumbed his nose at all human expectations of greatness, choosing humility underfoot as the most resplendent setting for the opening act of his grand redemptive work. In that moment, God's reputation in human eyes meant nothing. His saving purpose was all that mattered, and the result of that seemingly disreputable act has been greater glory than humanity could have ever imagined.

Weird, huh?

In that first breath, God redefined what glory is and means. He constructed a brand-new equation that only makes sense if God is truly God (which I believe he is). The new formula, to my mind, looks something like this:

Humility = Glory

This awkward, awesome equation that God demonstrated in his birth is something I struggle with, but which Agnes Bojaxhiu understood.

In case you're not familiar with Agnes, she was arguably the most beautiful woman of the twentieth century. No, she wasn't a supermodel or a princess—not a glamorous actress or a championship sports figure. Not even a pop star or a beauty-pageant winner. She was actually kind of homely (my opinion only). By the time I came to know her, she was a frail old woman, but I've seen pictures and I can tell you that she seems to have always looked old.

Still, let me describe Agnes, in her glory, for you.

She stood only four feet, eleven inches tall. She weighed less than a hundred pounds, and (to be honest) her face often resembled a shriveled prune. She never owned a home or a car or even so much as a closet full of clothes. As a nineteen-year-old girl, she took the name of Mary Teresa and dedicated herself to serving Jesus as a nun. Perhaps you know her best by the name she earned later in life, Mother Teresa.

And what did Mother Teresa do that made her the most beautiful person of the twentieth century? Simply this: she cared for the sick and dying.

She was called the "Saint of the Gutters" because she was always willing to help people the rest of the world despised. In her hometown of Calcutta, India, she often patrolled the neighborhoods looking for the "poorest of the poor," finding the terminally ill in the streets and literally carrying them from the gutters to Nirmal Hriday, her "home for the dying." There, she and her coworkers nursed these people so they could die with dignity.

Perhaps the best way to view the beauty of Mother Teresa is through the lens of a story from her life. The time was 1955. Leaving Nirmal Hriday, she once happened upon a Hindu priest outside her door. In the months prior, many Hindu believers in Calcutta had harassed Teresa and the other nuns assisting her, determined to oust these "sacrilegious" Christians from their city. They'd thrown stones and insults at the nuns and even threatened to kill them. By all rights, Mother Teresa should have harbored hatred toward Hindus, and particularly toward Hindu leaders like this priest.

But that day all Mother Teresa saw was a man. Lying on the pavement. Literally dying in his own vomit.

He was a victim of the deadly disease cholera. Because cholera is highly contagious, none of his fellow Hindu believers would touch him, gathering instead to form a crowd that watched in fascinated horror as this Hindu priest began to die an agonizing death.

Mother Teresa didn't hesitate. Pushing her way through the crowd, the little woman picked up the priest and carried him in her arms back inside Nirmal Hriday. There, she carefully placed him in a clean bed, then washed the refuse from his face and body. His death came soon after, but thanks to this Christian nun, the Hindu priest was allowed to die with dignity, his body clean and resting in a warm bed.

Each day of Mother Teresa's life contained these kinds of simple, selfless acts of beauty and service, so much so that when she died she was mourned by kings and commoners, princes and paupers alike. And because of her life in the gutters, we are all given a glimpse of the glory of Jesus Christ himself. For that reason I can think of no lovelier woman from the modern age, none who lived a life with more daily beauty than this little nun they once called Agnes.[8]

In her example I see a kindred spirit with the one who gave up residence in the heavens to make himself born under humiliating circumstances, in a humble city, in a degrading stable room. Humility, it seems, equals glory. Mother Teresa is testament to that. And Domenico di Pace Beccafumi. And, best of all, God himself.

God Transforms Everything He Touches

This past Christmas season in my part of the world has been filled with joy and splendor, lights and laughter, hope and even some measure of peace on earth.

And there were mangers everywhere.

Think about that.

Ancient animal troughs, so lowly and common in their day that farmers barely gave them a second thought, are now displayed with generous abandon all across the world. They are painted in gold, set up in lights, crafted from finest materials, bejeweled, designed by artists, and sold with retail markups—even though they'll never actually be used by any animal anywhere.

The manger is now surrounded by live performances, immortalized in fine art, displayed in front lawns, printed onto window clings that are pasted in children's rooms, and even used as a symbol before which Santa Claus himself prays.

A few millennia ago, that kind of treatment for a manger was not simply absurd; it was not even imagined. A manger was just what it was: a dirty tool, a makeshift box used for holding hay and feed, a place where barnyard animals took their dinner.

Today a manger is a symbol of nothing less than the glory of God himself. Why? Because it was touched by God incarnate; and God changes everything he touches, imbuing that thing with mischievous glory for all eternity.

You and I are like that manger. Before the touch of God, we're simply forgotten things used for base purposes. And then Jesus comes into our world, into our lives, into our homes and workplaces, and deeply into our souls.

We're touched by the Creator of glory, then we are changed, humble vessels hosting the King. Any greatness we may have thought we held is suddenly dwarfed into humility in the glare of his awesome presence. And any humble, degraded thing we may be is suddenly glorified by the awesome compassion of his instant, immediate, intimate love.

God transforms anything he touches. It was true of that manger so many centuries ago, and it's true in your life, in my life, today.

How sneaky of God: he welcomes us as we are—sinful, lost, helpless, debased—then he transforms each of us into heavenly children who radiate and enjoy his glorious presence now and forevermore.

Like the floor of the Duomo di Siena trodden underfoot

for centuries, like the humiliating incarnation of Christ into the underside of humanity, this life transformation God gives is a mischievous glory available to any who will see it for what it truly is. May we never lose sight of our Lord's greatness in this ridiculous regard—nor of his great love that works this sneaky glory into every breath we take.

TWO

MYSTERIOUS GRACE

It's a mystery.

—PHILIP HENSLOWE (PORTRAYED BY GEOFFREY RUSH),
IN *SHAKESPEARE IN LOVE*

For now we see through a glass, darkly.

—1 CORINTHIANS 13:12 KJV

The woman of Samaria had simply been going to get water. It was a mindless chore, really, and one she preferred to do alone. She'd waited until after the other women of her town had come and gone, then gathered herself around midday and walked out to the well just outside her hometown of Sychar. She didn't expect to find anything unusual on this chore, but there he was.

Sitting beside the well.

A Jewish rabbi. A member of the race that hated her half-breed heritage.

Waiting. Almost as if he was waiting for her.

Then, despite the social and cultural obstacles, despite the lack of invitation, he asked her for a drink. Like it was nothing! Like Jews and Samaritans did that every day. And as their conversation progressed, it went from unusual to bizarre.

"If you knew the gift of God," Jesus said to her, "and who it is that asks you for a drink, you would have asked him and he would have given you living water" (John 4:10).

What?

Were I to have been present, I would've been more than a bit confused by the enigmatic conversation going on at that well.[1] What at first seemed a commonplace moment (a trip to get water) was fast becoming a rush of secrets and—let's be honest—near absurdity.

The stranger who asked for a drink from the well was now claiming to possess some kind of mythical "living" water? Either he was crazy, or there was some great mystery of grace that he understood and the woman (and, subsequently, you and I) did not.

Ah, the mystery . . .

It's a Mystery

Life, especially when God is involved, is so often a mystery, isn't it?

One of my favorite commentaries on this comes from the 1998 movie *Shakespeare in Love*. In this Oscar-winning film, a young Will Shakespeare (played by Joseph Fiennes) struggles to complete his now-famous play, *Romeo and Juliet*. Alongside him, his benefactor and producer, Philip Henslowe (played by Geoffrey Rush), struggles to keep merciless creditors at bay long enough to debut young Will's new stage production. One particularly brutal creditor is Hugh Fennyman (Tom Wilkinson), a blackguard whose money-collection techniques include placing his debtors' feet into fires, cutting off noses and ears, and quite possibly murdering clients for nonpayment.

At a pivotal point in this film, a royal decree has been issued to shut down all theaters in London until further notice. That means Henslowe can't put on *Romeo and Juliet*, which in turn means he can't sell tickets to Shakespeare's new play, which means that it is now impossible for Henslowe to pay his debt to the sadistic Fennyman. And so it happens that, while walking peacefully through the marketplace, Henslowe suddenly finds himself in the clutches of Hugh Fennyman and his murderous henchmen.

"What have I done, Mr. Fennyman?" Henslowe stutters while being forcefully dragged across the square.

"The theaters have all been closed down by the plague," snaps Fennyman.

"Oh, that," says Henslowe.

"By order of the Master of the Revels," Fennyman says, emphasizing the severity of the shutdown and noting its royal source.

"Mr. Fennyman," says Henslowe, pausing just long enough to endure being slammed up against a hard wooden beam, "allow me to explain about the theater business. The natural condition is one of insurmountable obstacles on the road to imminent disaster."

"So what do we do?" asks Fennyman.

"Nothing," says Henslowe. "Strangely enough, it all turns out well."

"How?" Fennyman seethes.

"I don't know," says Henslowe. "*It's a mystery.*"

At that moment, a bell rings in the square and a royal herald walks past shouting the newest development: "The theaters are reopened by order of the Master of the Revels! The theaters are reopened!"

While his captors stand with open mouths, staring in wonder at the new turn of events, Henslowe gently extricates himself from their clutches and happily walks away with a promise that Shakespeare's play is soon to be ready.[2]

It's a mystery . . .

Those words ring true for so much of my life. Granted, I don't often have to face down bloodthirsty debt collectors the way poor Mr. Henslowe did, but my wife and I do often find ourselves face-to-face with the normal worries and threats of modern living. When we find ourselves in some new calamity of health or career or parenthood or family or finances or spiritual disruption, I often throw up my hands and seethe, *So what do we do now, God?*

And at the oddest times, during prayer or worry or both, for some reason this silly scene from a Hollywood love story pops into my head. I can almost hear God laughing behind the tones of Geoffrey Rush's voice.

Nothing, the soul-whisperer says to my disconcerted heart. *Strangely enough, it all turns out well. My grace is enough.*

I expect that when Christ started babbling about living water, the woman at the well felt a little like poor old Henslowe and me—confused and at a loss for what to do or expect next.

An interesting sidelight to the mystery of this moment for the woman at the well lies in Jesus' initial, unexpected request for water, and then in the mysterious suggestion of living water that he offered in return. Bible historians tell us that in the Middle Eastern culture of Jesus' day, "one of the first things done for a guest was to give him a drink of cool water. It was a pledge of friendship."[3]

In that cultural context, one has to wonder if by asking for a drink of water, Jesus was also asking for a pledge of friendship from this woman. By revealing that he had living water to give, was he also offering to this woman a pledge of eternal friendship? Did this woman at the well understand that an eternal friendship was being offered and requested? It's possible, but given the out-of-the-blue element of this particular situation in her life, I'm guessing it's not likely that she picked up all these theological nuances. At least not at that moment.

You see, while staring into the face of Christ, this woman was actually looking into the eyes of the universe's greatest mystery, of the one whose mere existence was beyond anything she could ever hope to understand or imagine. And strangely enough, it all turned out well for this woman, almost as if God, in his grace, had planned it that way.

We Need Mystery in Life

I suspect it's no accident that Jesus used the element of mystery in order to draw in the woman at the well. After all, he is God, and he knew two thousand years ago what educators and behavioral experts could not verify until recently: human nature loves a mystery.

Think of it this way. Let's say you and I are standing in front of a table. On the table are three boxes. Two of the boxes have clear plastic lids that allow you to see what's inside. There's a diamond necklace in one box and an extravagant emerald ring in the other. The third box is wrapped like a Christmas present and is about the same size as the other two boxes.

"Each box on this table, including the gift-wrapped one, is valued at ten thousand dollars," I say to you. "Now, as my gift, you can choose any one of these boxes to have as your own. The contents of that wrapped box will remain unseen unless you choose that as your gift. You have ten minutes to make your decision."

Over the course of the next ten minutes, which of these three boxes will you spend the most time inspecting?

If you're like the rest of us, you'll look admiringly at the diamond necklace and emerald ring, but you'll spend the bulk of your time carefully examining the gift-wrapped box, shaking it, feeling its weight in your hands, pressing its sides, checking for any tears in the wrapping paper, maybe even sneaking a quick sniff to see if you can solve the mystery of what's inside that last box. And, at the end of ten minutes (unless you have an overriding attraction to diamonds or emeralds), you will most likely choose the gift-wrapped box. Why? Because even though you like diamonds and emeralds, you, simply by virtue of the fact that you are human, have an ingrained attraction to the mystery represented by that gift-wrapped box. In short, your curiosity will overrule your knowledge, driving you to feel that you *must* know what is hidden inside that last box.

This kind of experience is what some scientists and marketing gurus call the "gap theory of curiosity." According to behavioral economist George Loewenstein of Carnegie Mellon University, curiosity is the result of noticing a gap in our knowledge—a gap that subsequently causes us intellectual pain, like an itch that needs to be scratched. In order to alleviate that intellectual itch, we strive to fill the gap with more knowledge, thus satisfying our curiosity and solving our intellectual mysteries.[4]

Marketing strategists Chip and Dan Heath explored Loewenstein's theory and applied it to the way we consume modern media. Listen to their insightful commentary:

> We sit patiently through bad movies, even though they may be painful to watch, because it's too painful not to know how they end. . . .
>
> Most local news programs run teaser ads for upcoming

broadcasts. The teasers preview the lead story of the evening, usually in laughably hyperbolic terms: "There's a new drug sweeping the teenage community—and it may be in your own medicine cabinet!" "Which famous local restaurant was just cited—*for slime in the ice machine*?" . . .

These are sensationalist examples of the gap theory. They work because they tease you with something that you don't know—in fact, something that you didn't care about at all, until you found out that you didn't know it.[5]

I would be reluctant to call Jesus a sensationalist (though some of his miracles might argue otherwise), but when I look at the conversation he initiated with the woman at the well, I can't help but feel that he was very much aware of what Loewenstein and the two Heaths would centuries later call the gap theory of curiosity.

"If you knew the gift of God," Jesus said to woman, "and who it is that asks you for a drink, you would have asked him and he would have given you living water" (John 4:10).

Do you see all the ways Jesus is teasing out the mystery of grace for this woman? The way he is drawing her to him with a hint of something she doesn't know—something that, really, she didn't care about at all until she found out she didn't know it? His one simple statement of fact so clearly reverberates with intellectual itches, creating questions that demand to be answered by the sudden gaps of knowledge inside her mind.

Do you know the gift of God?

Do you know just whom you are talking to?

What exactly is living water? Can there actually be such a thing?

And if there is such thing as living water, can this stranger really possess it—and give it away?

Even if he did have this water, how would he give it to me?

Just who is this strange man, anyway?

It's a mystery—and one that wasn't lost on this curious, thirsty woman.

"Sir," she said in response, "you have nothing to draw with and the well is deep. Where can you get this living water? Are you greater than our father Jacob, who gave us the well and drank from it himself, as did also his sons and his livestock?" (John 4:11–12).

Knowing what you now know about human nature, does it surprise you at all that this woman's immediate reaction to the mystery of Christ's words was to ask questions that would fill her knowledge gap? "Where can you get this . . . ? Are you greater than our father Jacob . . . ?"

And knowing what you know about Christ, would you be surprised to find out that those were the kinds of questions he wanted her to ask in the first place? Questions about his heavenly authority ("Where can you get this . . . ?") and his eternal identity ("Are you greater than our father Jacob . . . ?")—these were gaps in her knowledge that she didn't even know she'd had before she met this divine stranger at the well.

Had it been me, I'm pretty sure I would've played Jesus' cards differently. I mean, he knew what she needed to know, and knew that she needed to know it. So I probably would have marched up to this woman and said, "Hello, my name is Jesus Christ. I am the Son of God and your Messiah. You may now dedicate your life to me so that I can fill your thirsty soul with spiritual, living, eternal water."

Of course, had it been me in that position, this woman's story would likely have ended there! As the Heath brothers point out, we are too quick to simply download facts to others, when what they really need first is to *realize that they need these facts.* "The trick to convincing people that they need our message, according to Loewenstein, is to first highlight some specific knowledge that they're missing. We can pose a question or puzzle that confronts people with a gap in their knowledge. We can point out that someone else knows something they don't."[6]

Now I don't mean to suggest that Jesus tricked the woman at the well into belief. Still, it does seem apparent that Jesus had a thorough knowledge of human nature, of our intense curiosity in the face of a mystery, and that he was comfortable *becoming* that mystery in order to reach this woman with the news of his soul-quenching, living water. Why would he do this? Well, the most obvious reason to me seems to be that he liked it.

God Loves a Mystery

In this age of scientific discovery and intense theological study, sometimes it's easy to overlook the truly mysterious aspect of God's eternal personality and grace.

I have to smile when I read the apostle Paul's writings in the New Testament because even though he was arguably the world's first Christian theologian, he still thought Jesus was a never-ending mystery of deity and humanity. In his letter to the Colossians, Paul said his purpose was to help others "in order that they may know the mystery of God, namely, Christ . . ." and he asked his readers to pray for him and his companions "so that we may proclaim the mystery of Christ" (Colossians 2:2; 4:3). In his first letter to the Corinthians, he readily admitted, "Now we see a dim reflection, as if we were looking into a mirror, but then [when Christ returns] we shall see clearly. Now I know only a part, but then I will know fully, as God has known me" (1 Corinthians 13:12 NCV). Or as the classic King James translation poetically renders Paul's words, "Now we see through a glass, darkly . . ."

At the same time, I often feel sad when I hear my fellow Christians today pontificate on their knowledge and understanding of the mysteries of God. Not long ago my pastor preached a sermon on the Trinity—the theological idea that God is one person and at the same time is Father, Son, and Holy Spirit. During the sermon, he made a statement that while the Trinity is true, it can never be fully understood in this lifetime.

Afterward, a friend of mine casually belittled my pastor's statement, saying, "I've been studying the Bible for decades, and I understand everything there is to know about the Trinity."

My friend, it seems, has missed out on the breathtaking mystery of God and replaced it with her own limited understanding. I applaud her desire to study Scripture and to fill knowledge gaps as best she can, but I'm saddened she doesn't understand that her studies now are simply cliff-hangers in the mystery of eternity. Our God is not one who is easily explained or gently dissected into understandable sections. If there is one thing I've learned, it's that God will not be defined or limited by our expectations.

God, it seems, loves a mystery.

If you don't believe me, just read his book, the Bible, to see what I mean. In chapter 1 of Genesis you'll find an eternal, self-existent, all-powerful being, someone in need of absolutely nothing. And yet, he created. He spoke and everything that exists was formed—from the awe-inspiring, mammoth sun that warms our solar system to the mitochondria that inhabit your very cells.

Why would God do that? He had no need. He was not lonely or wishing for a friend. He needed no new hobbies—and he certainly could foresee the heartache and sinfulness that would run rampant in his creation over time. So why create at all?

It's a mystery.

In the book of Job you'll discover God making what appears to be a wager with Satan—a devastating bet that literally unleashes all hell into Job's existence. Job has been a dedicated, righteous servant of God his entire life. Why would God orchestrate this kind of suffering for him? Job asked that question of God himself, and the answer he got was less than clear! Matter of fact, when God was finished with him, Job's response was this: "Surely I spoke of things I did not understand, things too wonderful for me to know" (Job 42:3).

Job's suffering? Also a mystery, even to the one who suffered it.

But perhaps the greatest mystery of all comes in the first chapter of Matthew, where God inserted his very being within the uterus of a poor young woman who bore not simply a son, but the actual Son of God. His love drove him to do that. But what of the height, the depth, the width, the expanse, the texture, and the heart of that love? Can that ever be understood? No, not in this life; and maybe not even in the next. Why?

It's a mystery.

And God, it seems, loves a good mystery. Continue reading the stories of Christ and you'll discover him scattering seeds of mysterious grace in just about everything he says and does—in his parables, in his sermons, in his confrontations with the religious elite, in his quiet moments with his followers, in his family, in his miraculous acts, in his death, burial, and resurrection, and more. It should be no surprise, then, that when God wanted to capture the attention of the woman at the well, he did what comes naturally to him. He spoke about a mystery—his mystery—and waited for her to respond.

"If you knew . . . who it is that asks you for a drink . . ."

In Life's Mysteries, We See Glimpses of God

I don't know all, or even most, of God's reasoning behind the way he fills our lives with mystery. There is one thing I've discovered about Christ, though, and his enigmatic ways, something that the woman at the well first discovered so many centuries ago.

In life's mysteries, we see glimpses of God.

When Christ first hinted at his true nature and spoke a few clues about streams of living water, only then did the woman at the well begin to unravel the mystery of Jesus. "Are you greater than our father Jacob?" she asked (John 4:12).

When I read her words I want to whisper in her ear, "Yes, now you're beginning to get it! Now you're on the right track!"

There are times in my life when I wish someone would whisper those words to me.

I am so very good at forgetting to squint deeply into the mysteries that weave themselves into my life. Several years ago I required unexpected surgery. Unfortunately, the surgery solved one health problem but created another: near-constant nausea. Imagine morning sickness, but feeling that way all day, every day. While doctors were sorting this out, I was sick in bed—for months. I was unable to work. The inflow of money dwindled while the flow of household and medical bills increased.

On top of it all, our old house was in serious need of painting. After getting several professional estimates (and laughing at the ludicrous idea that we'd be able to pay the painters), we gave up. My wife, bless her heart, took a flat tool from her toolbox and began scraping the old paint off all by herself while I lay in bed each day, all day, trying not to throw up (again).

Why me? I grumbled to God. *Why us? I don't deserve this illness, and Amy certainly doesn't deserve to be stuck out in the blazing sun scraping flakes of paint off an old, beat-up house all by herself.*

But God didn't answer. Instead, he left us to face the mystery in silence.

Four days later, barely half of one side of the house was scraped (and that was one of the short sides of the house). It wasn't that our house was so big. It's just that it was a big job for only one person!

Then on the fifth day, just after dinner, cars began to drive up to the house. Friends of ours from church piled out wearing old clothes and with scrapers in hand. Ladders were unloaded, cans of primer were opened, and within two hours the entire house was scraped and primer had been spread over all the exposed areas. Wow!

But that's not all. A few days later, on a beautiful Colorado Saturday when people should have been boating at the lake, playing at a park, or hiking in the mountains, cars showed up at our house again and the painting began in earnest. These friends were so generous that they gave their time twice for this chore. They even brought the paint, the paintbrushes, and other supplies needed for the job. Then, just to rub it in I guess, they gave us a gift of money they'd collected for us to help out with the mounting tide of bills sitting unpaid on my kitchen counter.

At the end of the day, brushes were washed out, tired muscles were stretched, and everyone stood back to admire the house coated in new shades of blue.

What an incredible and tangible expression of grace in the family of God! When one member was weak, others were strong. Our neighbors were amazed too. Who was this group of people who cheerfully laughed and joked while swinging paintbrushes all day? Why were they doing this? These questions opened the doors for us to tell our neighbors how Christ himself had motivated these wonderful friends of ours.

When I was sick in bed, when our family finances were strained to the breaking point, when the best my wife had to offer was simply much too little and much too late, we were living in one of God's mysteries. I can't say I really liked living that experience, but I can say that when all was said and done, I caught a glimpse of God in the laughing, friendly faces of our friends. I saw a glimpse of Jesus in the sweaty, paint-splattered T-shirts they wore, and in the cool blue shade on the side of my house.

You see, it's often in the mysteries of life, in the moments and experiences that just seem to make no sense that we, like the woman at the well, are treated to a little glimpse of heaven.

Eventually my health improved enough for me to begin working again. The story could end there, but there's one last bit to be told.

Nearly a year later, my wife was looking through the papers our then-school-aged son had brought home from a Bible class. There was a take-home sheet titled "Helping Hands," and on it the instructions read, "Write a way you might help others when you grow up." On this handout Tony had drawn a picture of himself painting a house the exact shades of blue his home now was, and he had written, "Help paint somebody's house."

Fast-forward about seven years or so to when Tony was getting ready for high school. He had the opportunity to go on a short-term mission trip with the church youth group. He did the fund-raisers and went to all the training meetings. Got into a van and drove for a day and a half with a bunch of sweaty kids and devoted leaders. Slept on the floor of a school, gathered with other teens, sang songs to Jesus, held hands with other kids and prayed, and worked his heart out serving others.

Tony helped paint somebody's house.

I still remember lying in bed, vomit bucket reliably beside me, listening to my wife outside, scraping infinitesimal flakes of paint. I remember the sorrow I felt at hearing my son come home from school and not being able to throw a football with him in the backyard, not being able to attend his sporting events, barely being able to play board games with him before bed. I remember complaining to God about how unfair and unkind he was being to my family and me—and believe me, I complained a lot.

I just didn't realize that God had cast me in one of his glorious mysteries.

I didn't understand that we would all catch a glimpse of Jesus as a result of this situation, or that it would be an image my son would remember—and seek to imitate—for years to come.

If someone had taken me aside and whispered in my ear, "Hush, Mike. Strangely enough, it all turns out well," they would've been right. But I needed the mystery, the not knowing, to fully grasp the lesson. We all need gaps in our knowledge about God if we want to truly understand.

To be honest, I probably would have been skeptical, and it's likely I would have responded sarcastically and said, "Right, and how's that supposed to happen?" But I know now what the answer would have been:

It's a mystery.

THREE

CRIMINAL KINDNESS

God is constantly calling us to be more than we are, to see through plastic sham to living, breathing reality, and to break down our defenses of self-protection in order to be free to receive and give love.

—MADELEINE L'ENGLE[1]

If anyone is in Christ, he is a new creation.

—2 CORINTHIANS 5:17 HCSB

G eorge's life of crime started in 1962, when he met Walter Patterson.

Walter's daughter, Ann, was only fourteen years old then, just a few days shy of her birthday. On the day after Thanksgiving, after a warm family meal, she stood in a messy kitchen and watched through the window as her daddy climbed into his 1958 Chevy pickup. He was heading to work the night shift at the gas station he leased over in Collingwood Park, New Jersey.

Before Ann Patterson turned fifteen, her daddy would be dead.

It was right around 9:30 p.m. when George Wright met Walter Patterson. George wore a brown seamless stocking over his face and carried a .22-caliber rifle. His buddy, a guy named McGhee, brandished a revolver. They walked into Mr. Patterson's gas station and demanded money. When he objected, they beat the older man until he was bloodied and senseless, until he finally gave up all the cash he had: seventy dollars in crumpled bills. As a thank-you, McGhee shot him at point-blank range, sending a bullet through his liver and kidney until it imbedded in the old guy's hip. Walter slumped to the floor, bleeding.

They left Ann's daddy groaning on the ground.

After all that excitement, George was hungry. So he went out to dinner. Ate two cheeseburgers. Played shuffleboard. All the while knowing he'd left a man wounded and dying, just so he could get half of seventy dollars.

Two agonizing days later, Walter Patterson died in a hospital bed.

George Wright was arrested and eventually sentenced to fifteen to thirty years in prison for his role in the robbery and murder of Walter Patterson. That was too long for this angry young man, so he connected with a few other cons and broke out, hot-wiring the warden's car as the means of escape. He joined the Black Panthers, stayed under the radar, stayed on the run. Then on July 31, 1972, nearly ten years after the killing of Mr. Patterson, Mr. Wright became a domestic terrorist. The ex-con, fugitive, Black Panther hijacked Delta flight 841 heading from Detroit to Miami. Crazy thing is, he pulled it off, escaping to Algeria with a million dollars in cold, hard cash (though the Algerian government conveniently relieved him of that money soon after arrival).

From there, he began a worldwide fugitive odyssey that took him to Germany, France, Guinea-Bissau, and finally Portugal. Along the way, George changed his name to Jorge, and somewhere in the years between then and now, miraculously, Jorge became a different man.

"I've asked God to forgive me," he says now of his criminal past, "and I think God has forgiven me. But the law—the law says other things."

With Christ's forgiveness in his life, Jorge married. Had kids. Joined Grace Church and was baptized in the Atlantic Ocean.

He turned from crime, working with his hands to provide for his family. He volunteered for a Portuguese charity called Serve the City. He cleaned graffiti in Lisbon and helped to renovate an outreach center for HIV-positive children. He served dinners for homeless people. He planted public flower gardens. He raised two healthy, happy kids. He grew into a senior citizen, and in the forty years of his hiding, he didn't do anything to add to his crimes—not even a parking violation.

On September 26, 2011, the law finally caught up with George Wright in the form of six Portuguese policemen acting on an Interpol warrant issued by the United States. They found George Wright, but they arrested José Luis Jorge dos Santos. In the ensuing extradition hearings, the central issue was not whether they'd arrested the right man but whether they'd arrested the *same* man. The question they were asking was this:

Can a man change?

Can Christ interrupting a career criminal's life actually make that kind of difference? Can it turn an angry, violent young man into a quiet, serving, humble father and a productive member of society? Can it turn murdering George into gentle Jorge?

The attorneys from the United States say no, of course not. George Wright is guilty regardless of what he calls himself today, regardless of how long he's been able to stay in hiding, regardless of how many plates he serves the hungry homeless. Justice demands that he return to the United States and pay for his crimes.

The attorneys in Portugal think differently.

"They don't even see him as George Wright," reporter Michael Finkel wrote. "He's Jorge Santos, and has been for years. George Wright no longer exists. How can you punish a man who doesn't exist?" In this case, the attorneys in Portugal have prevailed—for now at least.[2] But the issue still remains: *Can a man change?*

That's a question that was asked about a different criminal some two thousand years ago when Jesus marched into his life and spoke just two words: *Follow me.*

As far as we know, this crook was not an accomplice to murder, but like George/Jorge, he was guilty of other serious crimes: theft, hijacking of goods, criminal menacing, and, in the eyes of his contemporaries, treason.

Also like Jorge, he used a name change to at least partially obscure his criminal past. He began life as Levi (son of Alphaeus). But today, for the most part, Levi no longer exists. We know him only by the name he used to author his gospel of Christ: Matthew.

What makes George and Levi so interesting is that both their life stories split distinctly into two chapters: a criminal existence before meeting Christ and an absolutely transformed life after. George Wright of America, in the eyes of his new country, no longer exists. There is only Jorge Santos, citizen of Portugal.

Likewise, Levi son of Alphaeus has all but disappeared from history, leaving only Matthew, a citizen of heaven.

When Christ comes along, even the worst can change— even a fugitive killer, even someone as treasonously corrupt as Levi.

Luke recorded Levi's soul-changing moment in his gospel in Luke 5:27–32.[3] If you'll grant me a moment of "sanctified imagination," I'd like to take a closer look at that story. I'd like to try to see it in my mind's eye, to witness the real man living a real moment in history. I picture it looking something like this.

Two Words

Levi wiped the sweat forming on his forehead, never noticing that the dust and dirt accumulating on his hand left a dark smear across the line of his right eyebrow.

"More," he said firmly, never taking his eyes off the stack of coins that teetered pleasingly on the table in front of him.

"Please," the merchant said piteously, "I have five children and a sick wife. We truly can spare no more!"

The smudge above Levi's eyebrow arched in appraisal. He quickly calculated the value of the silver coins in front of him. There was enough to pay the Romans, all right. But barely any left over to line Levi's silken pockets. A man of his position had expenses, and this merchant had to pay his part. After all, it was the merchant who had packed his carts with spices and salt meant for sale in Levi's precious Capernaum. He stood to profit from entry in this city. It was only fair that Levi also share in that profit.

He licked his lips, feeling the dryness and tasting the familiar grime of the day.

Besides, Levi didn't like this prattling trader. Didn't like anyone, really. That was one drawback of collecting taxes as a customs agent for King Herod and the Roman oppressors. It inevitably made you an enemy of those who put patriotism above a wealthy lifestyle. And it seemed as though there was an endless supply of those distasteful people. Well, they didn't like him, so he returned the favor.

"More."

The merchant laid four more coins on the table, wailing all the time that Levi would make him bankrupt—or worse. It was enough, all that Levi had asked for, actually. But now the glint of silver and the irritation of enduring this man's ceaseless whining took control.

"And a tenth of the cinnamon on your cart."

"What? You wretched little thief! You've taken my money and now you wish to take my livelihood as well? Never! Pigs don't deserve cinnamon. Let them wallow in the dirt where they can eat their fill of refuse. You may hang me from the highest branch or crucify my children and I'll never pay you more than what I already have!"

Levi stood. "Hanging and crucifixion can be arranged," he said.

He made a motion toward two Roman soldiers guarding the entryway to the city gate. They strode toward the merchant, who now cowered in fear. One soldier drew his sword and swung the flat part of the blade against the merchant's right temple. He crumpled to the ground, whimpering.

Levi walked around the table and knelt close to the merchant's ear. "Now, dog, I will take 15 percent of your cinnamon. And two more silver coins. Unless you object?"

"N-no. I will pay. I will pay."

The soldiers laughed and returned to their post. As they passed, Levi pressed a silver coin into the palm of the leader, and then waited patiently while the trader unloaded his cinnamon into a storage area behind Levi's table.

"Next!"

Levi had no problem collecting taxes for the rest of that day.

It was at nighttime when the problems came. When his eyes were open, Levi could endure the hateful stares and whispered curses people shot his way. When his eyes were open he could spit on the insults and sneers his fellow countrymen heaped on him, ignore the way people called him a traitor and lumped those of his profession with murderers and thieves. Even a prostitute had a better reputation than a tax collector. But Levi had soon discovered that a man with money always has friends, always has admirers among those who love a little wealth, who like to get closer to it. Levi didn't need friends who were self-styled Jewish patriots; he didn't need praise from the masses or even a country to call his own. All he needed—all he wanted—was enough capital to live comfortably and to punish his enemies.

Still, it was at night when life became difficult—when the sickly sweet smell of burning incense mixed with the memories of the day and when Levi lay down in his comfortable bed and finally let his eyelids close. That was when the voices calling him traitor changed to something more familiar, when the derisive faces and glaring hatred that oppressed his life reflected the feelings of Levi's own heart. In his nightmares, no matter how much money he tried to pay, the hardened face of his accuser would never relent, for that face was his own.

More than once his groans pierced the darkness.

"Oh, God! Who will save me from myself?"

But every morning the richness of his wine and the sumptuousness of his breakfast table made the agony of the night before fade. And so each day he took his position at the tax booth by the city's entrance, licking his lips, sweating in the grime, growing richer with every new "customer" who passed through.

It was on a day such as this that Levi discovered his true purpose in life. Already he'd collected a nice bounty of silver coins, flour, wheat, and even a smooth piece of ivory he couldn't resist. In his mind he was preparing for a party, a gathering of other tax collectors and "sinners" at his house to celebrate the wealth of his position. They were not true friends, of course. But they shared his fate and thus were more than happy to share his food when it was offered.

Then something of a commotion distracted Levi from exacting his taxes.

"It's the rabbi! He has come to Capernaum!"

Levi watched as onlookers in the marketplace rushed to get a glimpse of this rabbi. Certainly he wasn't worth losing out on silver and spices! He turned his attention back to the table and demanded two more coins. The merchant pleaded for mercy (they always did, it seemed), and Levi sighed.

Out of the corner of his eye he caught sight of a peculiar movement. Was the rabbi's procession going to pass right in front of this booth? Absurd! Levi had work to do, and while he respected many religious leaders, he would not allow any interruption in his accumulation of wealth.

Suddenly the air stilled around him. Silence fell over the marketplace and he felt as though all eyes had suddenly turned to him.

He looked up from the sparkling coins on his table and caught his breath.

A man—the rabbi—stood before him. It was not all eyes gazing on Levi; it was only the rabbi's eyes, and in them the tax collector could see heaven staring into his soul.

It was almost like nighttime again, there in the middle of the day. The accusing voices inside him breached their defenses and shouted *Guilty! Guilty!* in his ears. Memories of greedy theft and abuses of power flashed through his mind. The pain was nearly unbearable, and Levi wanted to cry out, to run from those eyes that pierced and convicted and shoved the unblinking truth out into the open.

"Who are you?" the tax criminal whispered, trembling in spite of himself.

The rabbi said nothing at first, only took a moment longer to gaze into his quarry's eyes. Then he smiled, and in the shadow of that smile Levi found erasure, heard the condemning voices being choked into silence, heard a new voice murmuring *Forgiven . . . forgiven . . . forgiven . . .*

The rabbi finally spoke.

"Follow me."

Two words, no more.

The rabbi waited.

Two words; that's all it took.

Two words that changed the destiny of a criminal, a traitor, a thief, a liar.

The world stopped in between the seconds ticking on the clock. Levi felt sudden hope swelling inside him. Anything. Everything. All of him. To follow him, no matter where, no matter when.

Matthew got up, left it all on the customs table—left it all behind.[4]

Why Does Christ Make a Difference?

In case you didn't catch it already, in the eyes of his Jewish contemporaries in ancient Israel, Levi the *telōnēs* (tax collector) was scum. A degenerate, traitorous reprobate. *Telōnēs*—a "tax collector universally hated throughout the Roman world because of inherent corruption." Charles Swindoll wrote: "Tax collectors had betrayed their people, rejected their heritage, despised their temple, and renounced their God. Tax collectors had sold themselves to foreigners, which put them on the same level as shameless harlots."[5]

It takes a unique kind of man to be that kind of man.

Someone a lot like George Wright, I think. A person dedicated only to himself, regardless of what that means for those around him.

Humorist Robert Benchley is credited with the observation that the world is divided into two types of people: those who divide the world into two types of people, and those who don't.[6] Well, at the risk of being classified with the first group Benchley describes, it's no stretch to say that during the time of Jesus in the land of Israel, there were two types of people: those who were patriots and those who were traitors. Levi was one of the traitors.

Religious leaders of Jesus' time didn't even try to reach out to redeem sinners like that; to do so would've been worse than embarrassing. A criminal like Levi doesn't change, so why even bother? A tax collector, by virtue of his soul-diseased profession, was considered ritually unclean, making him both unfit for religious activity and a contaminant to others who desired to participate in religious activity. Even the simple act of eating with a tax collector made a person unclean.[7]

And then Jesus Christ came along and spoke only two words:

"Follow me."

In that moment Levi *telōnēs* transformed into Matthew the apostle. Scripture seems to indicate he didn't even hesitate. He left behind his tax booth and never looked back. This from a man who had previously sacrificed his heritage, his temple, and even his country—simply to get rich as a tax collector. Levi had everything, but he still needed more. Now, suddenly, in the face of Jesus, all his wealth and power meant nothing to him. In the space between the seconds he walked away, abandoning everything he'd worked so hard to gain, just to follow this rabbi.

"Follow me," Jesus said.

It was an offer Levi couldn't refuse.

Why, I wonder? Why does Jesus make that kind of difference, even in the life of an unreachable reprobate like Levi, like Matthew?

Jesus explained it later that night, at a party at Matthew's house.

A great crowd of "tax collectors and sinners" were celebrating with Matthew and Jesus, eating and drinking at Matthew's plush home. A group of religious leaders came by. They were, understandably, offended to see Rabbi Jesus in that "unclean" mix of bad company. "Why do you eat and drink with tax collectors and sinners?" they complained.

That got Jesus' attention. I imagine him setting down his wine cup, leaning back in a chair and grinning.

"It is not the healthy who need a doctor," he said, "but the sick" (Luke 5:29–31).

Why does Jesus make a difference? Well, that's why: because the sick need a doctor.

When the human soul is steeped in sin and corruption and ungodly desire, it's like a terminal sickness that runs through every man or woman. The only hope for a cure from that deadly condition is Jesus Treatment—abandoning everything you have and want and trading it all in for the privilege of responding to Christ's call to Levi: "Follow me."

I have a silly kids' picture book that gives me a colorful image of what happens when this kind of radical, transformative interruption occurs in a life. It's called *The Napping House*, by Audrey and Don Wood.

In this little story, an entire family is apparently overcome by some mysterious sleeping sickness that rules human and animal alike. In the napping house, a snoring granny is caught in impenetrable sleep, soon joined by a dreaming child, a dozing dog, a snoozing cat, and a slumbering mouse. Outside the world is dark and rainy; inside everyone is lost in the fog of deep, deep sleep.

In the shadows of the house, only one living thing is awake: a tiny flea on the back of the slumbering mouse.

So Dr. Flea does what it must do: it bites the mouse.

That sets off a chain reaction! The mouse jumps awake, which scares the cat awake, which then claws the dog awake, which then thumps the child awake, who bumps the granny awake. Outside, the sun at last begins to break through the shadows, light streams through the windows, and a rainbow forms over the home. Finally, they all shake off their slumber and rise in delirious joy to greet the beautiful afternoon, "In the napping house, where no one now is sleeping."[8]

Jesus, of course, is not a flea, but his call to Levi caused a similar kind of chain reaction in the tax collector's heart. Levi's soul was caught in a sickening, slumbering darkness of his own sin, unable to rise into the light that awaited him. Christ's call jolted his soul awake, a radical spark that caused him to open his eyes and finally see the bright new vision of life God had planned for him from the beginning.

Why did Jesus make a difference in Levi's life? Because Levi was sin-sick and in need of the Doctor of our souls. Only Jesus could see Levi's true destiny. Only God in the flesh could communicate that life-saving vision for Matthew, for his health, wholeness, and future. And he did it with only those two words: *follow me.*

Why Does Christ *Not* Make a Difference?

In his book *The Element*, Ken Robinson tells the story of Gillian Lynne. Today Ms. Lynne is a world-famous dancer and choreographer, and a millionaire. She collaborated with Andrew Lloyd Weber on *The Phantom of the Opera* and *Cats*. She was a soloist with the London Royal Ballet and performed in countries all over the planet. And she's the founder of her own musical theater company that produces lauded shows in New York and abroad.

But as a child, she was simply Gillian, the kid who couldn't sit still—the girl with a learning disability and a bleak future. She was the problem child destined for, well, not much.

Then, one day, Gillian's mother took her to a new doctor, a psychologist who could see beyond the symptoms in the little girl's life and into her bright future. After talking with mother and daughter for a while, the psychologist took mom into the hallway to continue the conversation privately.

"Mrs. Lynne," the doctor said, "Gillian isn't sick. She's a dancer."

Suddenly little Gillian was given a glimpse of who she really was, what she was really meant to do. It was a siren call for her life, and it made all the difference. Gillian's mother enrolled her daughter in dance classes and the rest, as they say, is history.[9]

This, I believe, is the kind of thing that happened to Levi

while he was sitting at his tax collector's booth. Jesus came by and said, "You are not who you think you are, not what everyone has said you are. You are no crook and traitor. You are my disciple. You are my friend. You are no longer Levi; you are Matthew. Now follow me."

That vision, that reality, that call from the mouth of heaven—it changed Levi. It made an unimaginable difference.

When I see the radical transformation that happened in that one glorious moment in the life of Matthew, I'm filled with wonder and awe . . . and disappointment.

Jesus came along, and Matthew was changed forever, yet many people today claim to have had similarly radical encounters with the resurrected Christ, but it doesn't seem to have made a difference at all in their lives.

Why, I wonder? Why did Jesus make a difference for Levi, but not for many who call his name today?

Jesus might have offered the explanation when he spoke to the Pharisees about their disapproval of his choice of Levi: "It is not the healthy who need a doctor, but the sick" (Luke 5:31). Why doesn't Jesus make a difference in the lives of some? *Because they don't believe they're sick.* They think they don't need a doctor. They use a warped logic of righteousness that blinds them from seeing the true, life-giving vision that Jesus has for them. As Brennan Manning has said, "It is not the prostitutes and tax collectors who find it more difficult to repent: it is the devout who feel they have no need to repent."[10]

Dr. Martin Luther King Jr. faced this kind of twisted logic nearly every day of his life. "Someone formulated the argument for the inferiority of the Negro . . ." he said, and it went like this:

All men are made in the image of God;

God, as everyone knows, is not a Negro;

Therefore, the Negro is not a man.

The logic of this syllogism is sound, but the vision it delivers is full of disease! Said Dr. King, "So men conveniently twisted the insights of religion, science, and philosophy to give sanction to the doctrine of white supremacy. . . . And men then embraced this philosophy . . . They sincerely came to believe the Negro was inferior by nature."[11]

This is the warped thinking of a soul-sick person—one who desperately needs the healing transformation of Jesus, but who refuses to admit the need for a doctor. These are people blinded to the real vision that Christ brings when he says, "Follow me," replacing it instead with their own logical fallacies of religious devotion and misunderstanding.

Where Jesus sees the dancer, they see only disability.

Where Jesus sees the disciple, they see only a crook.

Where Jesus sees the man, they see only the subhuman.

Why doesn't Jesus make a difference? Because the sick need a doctor—and sometimes, often really, they refuse to admit they're sick. It's a mistake of vision, a warping of our ability to see or even glimpse Christ's discipling call and purpose for our lives. And it's the reason we Christians are so often un-Christlike in the way we live, the way we love, and the way we represent our master to the culture in which he's placed us.

In my own life, I've found that Christians are the people who most often make themselves my bitterest enemies, who are most hurtful toward my family and me, who are most ready to lump me in with tax collectors and sinners. I've found them in churches, in Christian homes, in Christian colleges and Christian businesses, and even in Christian bookstores. And they've been pretty good about finding me as well!

I used to save the hate mail I got from readers, but it was too depressing—not because I believed it but because it always left me wondering why Christ hadn't made a difference in those people's lives. I used to suffer whenever another Christian told me how awful I was, or how much of a screwup I was, or how I was undeserving of his Christ. Now I just sigh and move on. Believe me, I've heard it all before.

Suffice it to say that I have, at various times, been condemned to hell (alongside C. S. Lewis, so I figured that was at least pretty good company). I've been called a tool of Satan, been censored and insulted and blocked from positions of leadership. I've been lied about, lied to, and cheated. I've had my tires slashed, been publicly ridiculed, verbally abused, stolen from, and threatened with physical violence. I've been blamed for the decline of modern civilization. I've been called both too Christian and not Christian enough. I've been called arrogant trash and a big jerk. I've been told I was too focused on the Bible and, simultaneously, that I was not focused enough on the Bible. I've been told I was too liberal and at the same time been shunned for being too conservative. I've been told I was an embarrassment to Jesus and that I couldn't possibly be Christian at all. I could go on, but I'm guessing you get the idea.

What's truly hurtful about all these insults is that they all came from Christian people, many of whom were—and still are—respected leaders in the Christian community.

As I look at that list now, I must be honest and tell you that I probably deserve at least some of that criticism—maybe all of it. And it may be that there are people out there who would see in me the same kind of hurtfulness I've just condemned in others. The reason is obvious because like Levi, I, too, am sin-sick and in constant, desperate need of soul healing. So before I go too far in accusing my brothers and sisters for their impoverished vision of Christ-life, I suppose I must take my gaze away from my window and turn it squarely into my mirror: *Why doesn't Jesus make a difference in my life? Or at least a more noticeable difference?*

I suppose it must be because sometimes, most times, I hear Christ calling and I say to myself, *He's talking to someone else. After all, it's the sick who need a doctor, and surely I'm not sick, am I?*

It makes me wonder. If I'd been that crook who sat at Levi's tax table and Jesus himself walked up to me with the command, "Follow me," what—really—would I have done?

What If Levi Had Said No?

I like to think that in Levi's situation, I'd have done my best imitation of a Mexican jumping bean and leapt out of my chair, leaving everything behind me to gain everything before me in the person of Jesus Christ.

I don't know if I would have, though.

I am someone who so easily, and so regularly, misses the mark. Just ask anybody in my family. Thankfully, Jesus didn't find me collecting taxes for Caesar (and stealing a little for myself). He found Levi. I'm so grateful that Levi said yes to Jesus' call!

But what if he'd said no?

We know that Levi had mortgaged himself to gain a substantial portion of wealth in his world. We know that when Christ came calling, he was forced to choose between that poverty of riches and the richness of poverty with Jesus. We know that leaving his position as a tax collector meant Matthew could never go back to it—Herod and the others in Roman civil government would be unlikely to allow that.[12] So it was all or nothing for Matthew—and he chose the all to be found in having nothing but Jesus. And then what?

History and tradition tell us that after Jesus' resurrection Matthew spent about eight years preaching in and around his home territory of Judea in Israel. After that, it's believed that he took the message of Jesus to Arabia, Syria, and Ethiopia. Somewhere in there, likely around AD 70, while in Syria, Matthew put down the stories of Christ in written form, sealing his place in history and creating for us a record that would literally lead millions and millions to faith. He finally suffered a martyr's death, being killed by the sword while preaching in Ethiopia.[13]

Can you imagine the void in history—and to your own personal experience with Jesus—if Levi the tax collector had said no when the Messiah called? If he'd chosen personal riches in place of spiritual ones? If he'd kept his money and instead bankrupted the vision God kept for him? Saying no to Christ's visionary call on a life has enormous consequences—and Levi would have never even seen the true cost of his greed in that circumstance.

It makes you wonder.

Sometimes, in the dim hours just before morning, I find

myself dreaming, half-awake, half-lost in the semitiredness of the dawn. I see myself seated at Matthew's table, faced with that unavoidable Savior who calls to me, day after day.

"Follow me," he says.

"Where?" I ask.

"Does it matter?" he says. "Follow me."

"When?" I stutter.

"Now. Five minutes from now. All day long. Follow me."

"What if I can't? What if I fail?"

"Follow me."

"I'm not good enough."

"Follow me."

"I'm afraid it might hurt. That it'll cost me everything."

"Follow me."

And I wake up, staring at the ceiling, his words still echoing. *Follow me.*

In that moment, the world stops in between the seconds ticking on the clock. I feel a sudden hope swelling inside me. The morning begins and I know I can't stay where I am, not for long. I have many questions. I have many worries. I have many flaws and many empty dreams. And still I hear him saying, "Follow me."

So, I finally get out of bed, *and . . .*

FOUR

FRIGHTENING WONDER

*The glory of the mildest show of the Living One is
such, that even the dearest of his apostles, the best
of the children of men, is cowed at the sight.*

—GEORGE MACDONALD[1]

*They were terrified and asked each other, "Who is
this? Even the wind and the waves obey him!"*

—MARK 4:41

t all started with a cotton swab.

That's it, really.

Dr. Mohan Korgaonkar was the surgeon, and Dr. Kwok Wei Chan was assisting as the anesthesiologist. The nurse stood vigilantly nearby. The patient, an elderly woman, was pleasantly snoring on the operating table. So there they were, Dr. Korgaonkar, Dr. Chan, the nurse, a long-suffering patient, and the cotton swab.

The date was October 24, 1991, and all was going as planned. An operation was scheduled and underway at the Medical Center of Central Massachusetts in Worcester, Massachusetts. Dutifully doing his job, Dr. Chan administered the anesthesia, sending the patient into a deep, sense-free slumber. With a confidence that comes from more than two decades of experience, Dr. Korgaonkar deftly began the procedure. All was going well.

Except, it seems, for our two physicians. No one knows for sure what words passed between them, but the intent was clear. These men didn't like each other.

Silently the minutes ticked by, and with each passing moment the tension in the operating room grew thicker. And thicker.

Perhaps Dr. Chan was a "backseat surgeon," offering unwanted advice about the ongoing operation. Perhaps Dr. Korgaonkar told a belittling joke about anesthesiologists in general, or about Dr. Chan in particular.

Whatever the reason, at one point during the operation, Dr. Chan muttered a profanity in the surgeon's direction. Almost without thinking, Dr. Korgaonkar flicked a cotton-tipped prep stick disdainfully at the anesthesiologist. Apparently, the surgeon had a good aim, because that tiny cotton swab hit its target and sparked everything that happened next.

Dr. Chan retaliated.

First came shoving. Then shouting. Then an all-out brawl between the two learned men of medicine. Fists flying and surgical goals forgotten, the doctors escalated into a wrestling, punching, jabbing, name-calling bout on the operating room floor.

And our patient? She slept through it all. Thank God.

Finally the two men tired a bit, regained their composure, got up, and finished the operation, only marginally worse for the wear. Not long after, each was fined $10,000 by the state Board of Registration in Medicine and ordered to submit to joint psychotherapy for their aggressive tendencies.

And to think, it all started with a cotton swab.[2]

It just goes to show, I suppose, how quickly this life can warp out of our control. Or really, how little control we actually have!

Dr. Korgaonkar's patient had no idea of the potentially life-threatening battle that raged around her while she slept. The nurse on duty was helpless in the face of that storm and could do little more than monitor the patient's vital signs while the two men went to war beside her. And then it was suddenly over, and the world moved on almost as if nobody had noticed.

I have an idea that kind of out-of-control feeling happens more often in life than we'd like—and more intensely than we admit. This can be especially frustrating for people of faith because we know our God is involved in those moments. And let's face it: he's never caught off guard by anything that happens to us. But when those life-shaking moments happen, he often seems not to notice —or not to care.

Now, before you accuse me of slander or blasphemy or whatever else that last sentence did to make you feel offended, I want you to know I'm not saying anything that Christ-followers haven't said for thousands of years.

Consider, if you will, a little event I like to call:

When God Was Sleeping

"Should we wake him?"

It was, in truth, more than just an awkward social situation.

It was nighttime, after a long, busy day. Jesus and his disciples had spent the morning and afternoon and into the evening in the company of a large crowd beside Lake Gennesaret, also called the Sea of Galilee.[3] All day long Jesus had taught the crowd, at one point even moving to preach from a perch inside a boat floating in the water simply because there was no more room for him on the shore.

"How can he sleep in this weather?"

Finally, after the sun eased into the horizon, Jesus and "the boys" were spent, both physically and mentally. But the crowd refused to leave. They were still hungry to hear more from this strange and wonderful floating rabbi.

"Let us go over to the other side," Jesus said at last to his closest friends, motioning toward the deep end of the sea (Mark 4:35). They were inclined to agree. Scripture tells us that "leaving the crowd behind, they took him along, just as he was, in the boat. There were also other boats with him" (v. 36).

And there they were, nighttime now in full bloom, a small flotilla of fishing boats slowly making their way across the Sea of Galilee. No surprise at this point: the Son of God was worn out. He did what any Son of Man would do; he curled up on a cushion in the stern of the boat and promptly fell asleep. A deep, cavernous, sleep. He deserved it, after all. It had been a long day.

And then . . .

"A furious squall came up" (Mark 4:37).

Ah, life. Spinning wildly out of control. Unexpectedly. Again.

When I'm reading about this moment in Mark 4:35–41, it sounds a bit tame to me to read the words "furious squall" here. How quaint, right? Almost sounds like a cute little tantrum that a preschooler might throw after being denied a second cookie. What's the big deal with a little rain? We've all experienced thunderstorms, so really, how bad could this fussy little squall be?

Well, apparently "furious squall" is something of an understatement here. The better translation is "mega storm"!

Got your attention now? Fact is, the word Mark used that we translate as *furious* in the New International Version—or *great* in other Bible translations—actually is *mĕgas*. Yeah, that looks familiar, doesn't it? It means, "exceedingly great, high, large, loud, mighty, strong."[4]

What's more, this furious little tantrum appears to be much more than just a "storm." Mark's literal wording for *squall* here was *lailaps*—that is, "whirlwind."[5] Fellow gospel writer Matthew was even more emphatic when he described it, probably because he was actually there to experience this moment in history. Matthew called this furious storm a *mĕgas sĕismŏs*! If you live in California you've already figured out what that means. For the rest of us, here's a more literal translation: *mĕgas* ("exceedingly great, high, large, loud, mighty, strong") *sĕismŏs* ("earthquake").[6]

In other words, this furious storm is so severe, it's akin to a disturbance of tsunami-like proportions, bearing down relentlessly on a bunch of guys hanging out in little boats, just trying to get from one side of the lake to the other. Watching helplessly as the waves break high over their heads, taking on so much water that their sailing vessels are nearly swamped and sunk. This *mĕgas sĕismŏs* really happened. Because of it real men were in real danger, and guess what? God just took a nap.

It's not hard to imagine what the disciples must have been feeling out there in the middle of Lake Gennesaret, deep into the night, trying to cross over. A few fragile boats caught in this perfect storm. Men watching Jesus sleep while the world washes away before their very eyes. You can almost hear the terror in each disciple's voice as it mingles with the anger of stinging wind and rain.

"Should we wake him?"

"How can he sleep in this weather?"

"Watch out!"

"Stay down!"

You can almost feel the nausea-inducing lurches of the little boat as it dips and swamps in the seawater, struggling to stay afloat.

"Somebody has got to wake him—or we'll all die out here in this storm!"

You can almost taste the desperation. They are merely men, after all. Twelve of them—helpless, frightened, wet, and tired. Together, yet alone. God sleeps in the storm; it appears he's forgotten his most faithful followers. Left them to be swallowed up by the elements while he takes a little catnap at their expense.

You can almost see the despair as it etches itself in the faces of the twelve. How long will it be before anyone misses them? Before Peter's bloated body washes up on the shore? Or shattered planks left over from their broken boat tear a cursing fisherman's net? Before old Zebedee hears the news that his beloved sons, James and John, have tangled with the sky and the sea and lost their lives in the fury?

How long before someone has the courage to awaken the slumbering Savior?

You can almost smell the sky burning as lightning cracks close by, blinding the big men in the little boat, tipping some this way and others that way and driving all dangerously close to the edge of sanity. And finally, they can hold it in no longer: "Teacher, don't you care if we drown?" (Mark 4:38).

"Jesus, Jesus, please wake up! If ever we needed a Savior, it would be right now."

Finally the God-Man stirs, eyes flicking open to take in the tumult surrounding him, ears listening stealthily to the children who cry out before him. He is unsurprised and unafraid.

I'm guessing that after sleeping in a cramped boat during a furious squall, he might have stretched a bit to get a crick out of his neck. He probably looked at his disciples and then at the sky and waves around him. Then he stood up. (Warning to Jesus: you're standing up in a small boat being violently rocked during a deadly storm . . . but whatever—).

And he spoke . . . *to the waves* . . . as if reprimanding rambunctious children, as if the water could actually hear him and respond.

"Quiet! Be still!" (Mark 4:39).

A word, and the wind dies to nothing; a frown, and the rain sweeps away. In a moment, all is calm on the entire lake. Silence, interrupted only by the rapid beating of twelve awestruck hearts. And the words of the sleeper: "Why are you so afraid?" (Mark 4:40).

Jesus Is One Scary Dude

Are you kidding me, God?

Is Christ serious here? It's almost as if he's oblivious to the clear and present danger they are all in. "Why are you so afraid?" he asks, and I imagine myself sitting next to him in the boat, wanting to scream in all caps: "BECAUSE WE'RE ALL GONNA DIE A GRUESOME, CHOKING, WATERY DEATH IN THIS EXCEEDINGLY GREAT, HIGH, LARGE, LOUD, MIGHTY, STRONG, EARTHQUAKELIKE TSUNAMI OF DEATH!!"

But before I can get those words out, I realize the storm is suddenly, abruptly over.

And I suddenly find I'm having trouble breathing.

The howling wind weakens to the breaking point and dies away like a whimper. The boiling waters and Goliath-sized waves simply disappear. The night sea all around me is suddenly glassy and smooth. I don't know about you, but at that moment, if I'm one of Jesus' disciples, I'm thinking this: *That storm was scary. But Jesus is terrifying . . .*

That not only makes sense to me, it's what actually happened. Mark recorded the end of this story with these words: "They [the disciples] were *terrified* and asked each other, 'Who is this? Even the wind and the waves obey him!'" (Mark 4:41, emphasis added).

In case you didn't notice it last time you read this "Jesus Calms the Storm" story in your Bible, you should know something the disciples obviously recognized: Jesus is—in the best sense possible—one scary dude.

How awesome is that?

"They were terrified . . ."

Suddenly the disciples were more afraid of their Savior than they were of a killer storm! That used to confuse me, but as more and more gray hair appears in my beard, I'm beginning to understand.

If you and I are among the fortunate ones, there will inevitably be a rare moment that comes into life when we, like every follower of Christ, must stare into the face of Jesus and realize with joyous horror that we're seeing more than just our classic "gentle Jesus, meek and mild." In that moment, we must at some level reconcile the iconic image of our tender God with his arms outstretched as if waiting for a hug with the frightening reality that our Father is more than just Daddy—he's what Rich Mullins called our "Awesome God." The prophet Isaiah had a moment of clarity like that, and his instantaneous response was, "Woe to me! . . . I am ruined!" (Isaiah 6:5).

The disciples, soaking wet, beaten by the elements, worn out and exhausted, had a similar epiphany sitting in that little boat in the middle of the Sea of Galilee.

Even the wind and the waves obey him.

Doesn't that scare you, just a little bit at least?

Even the whirlwind quiets at his slightest frown.

Doesn't that unimaginable power make your insides tremble?

Even the sun dims or blazes at his command.
Even the breath you take right now is happening simply because he wills it to be so.

Doesn't that frighten you with the limitless wonder of his being?

Even the most chaotic, reckless, havoc-bringing storm in your life is subject to the whims of that guy who could sleep through anything. That worn-out Messiah who snored while his disciples feared they were going to drown.

I feel a kind of frightening wonder when I catch any rare glimpse of who Jesus really is, when I pause long enough to take a real, honest look at the God incarnate, who refuses to abandon me despite my constant failures and sin. Like Jesus' disciples, I watch impotently as events of my life spin dangerously out of my control (again)—yet I never slip out of God's hand. Jesus never promised I'd always be safe—only that he'd always keep me secure. That's actually frightening to me. And wonderful.

I feel that this must be something of what Joshua meant when he said, "Now, therefore, fear the LORD and serve Him in sincerity," and what the psalmist meant when he wrote, "You who fear the LORD, praise Him . . . stand in awe of Him" (Joshua

24:14 NASB; Psalm 22:23 NASB). It is both terrifying and exhilarating to serve our mighty God.

Of course, it's easy to say that last sentence here on dry land, in my warm, comfortable office and ergonomically correct chair. It's quite a bit harder to believe it when life's storms are raging out of control. Maybe you're like me. Maybe sometimes your life takes a wrong turn and suddenly you feel trapped like those twelve helpless men caught in a furious squall, sinking like dead weight in a flimsy lifeboat of your own design.

Maybe your job stinks, your boss is a wad, and your work is depressing; perhaps your health is failing, or your kids are causing you heartache, or your marriage is near its desperate end. Maybe you woke up this morning and just couldn't bring yourself to get out of bed, or maybe your destiny is to wake up tomorrow in the same prison cell where you awoke yesterday, trying to find meaning in a life that's lived behind bars. Maybe you're hungry because you just don't have enough money to buy groceries this week; maybe you're wishing you had a boss who was a wad and your work was depressing because that'd mean at least you had a job!

Maybe this life just hurts. Oh, not every day, but enough days to notice—and remember. And maybe you can't help but wonder sometimes why God is absent from your pain or oblivious to the clear and present dangers you face. You might never admit it out loud, but it feels as though God has fallen asleep on you, or worse, that he's stopped paying attention to your troubles. Perhaps, at night, you find yourself echoing the cry of Christ's disciples in the storm, "Master! Jesus! I'm going to drown in this sorrow!"

Take heart, friend. Your Savior is not helpless, nor is he absent or sleeping or inattentive to your out-of-control world. This is fact, regardless of your feelings.

Your Jesus is one scary dude. He controls wind and waves and even your very life. That may sometimes make you uncomfortable because he often seems to have different plans for his followers than you or I do. He might actually steer us into the storm, but we must always remember: Jesus' frightening wonder is only a true terror for anything and anyone that dares to harm the object of his love—you.

We Have Nothing to Fear but God Himself

I'm going to tell you a private story now—one that, up to this point, I've only shared with a few very close friends. I expect that some of you may disbelieve it, or explain it away, or simply reserve judgment and move on, and that's okay. I don't tell you this to convince you that it really happened, only to illustrate an important truth I'm still learning about the Christian life: "The LORD is my helper, so I will have no fear" (Hebrews 13:6 NLT).

When my son was younger, he was sometimes afraid to face basic situations in life. He was nervous, occasionally to the point of tears, about asking a salesclerk for help at a retail store. He was frightened to go into our basement, even though that's where his playroom—with a zillion toys—and our family TV room were located. In those times, I found that it was sometimes more important for him to be afraid of facing me—who loved him and would always stand near as his safety net—than to be afraid of facing, say, a dark basement or a friendly salesperson. The result? He learned how to face down his fears, and we both got to rejoice together with his growing confidence and every new success.

I tell you about my son because when I was thirty-three years old I had to learn, in a very hard way, a lesson similar to the one I taught him.

In January 1996 I came down with an illness that no doctor could explain. It must have been some kind of wicked flu virus or something like that because the symptoms were similar—but to an extreme. For three weeks I could barely move. I had a near-constant fever that hovered between 102 to 104 degrees. I felt agony from the bottom of my feet to the top of my head and everywhere in between. I've been sick many times before and after this experience—sometimes very sick—but never have I felt so physically ravaged as I did at this time.

Somewhere between the second and third week of this illness, I found myself lying in bed, feeling abject misery, wishing I could simply die and get it all over with. And then I started thinking about stories I'd read of people who "lost the will to live" and had actually died shortly after. I recalled how Jesus chose his moment of death, and how Stephen also had released his spirit into the arms of Jesus (John 19:30; Acts 7:59–60). Maybe I was delirious, but I decided that I wanted to do that too.

At that moment, my wife came in to check on me. She must have thought I was losing my senses because I asked her, "How do I release my spirit? How do I let myself go from here?"

I'm pretty sure I scared her. She put a cold rag on my forehead, told me to rest, and immediately ran into the other room to call her mother, a nurse, for help. I heard her speaking on the phone. "Mike is *not* well," she said. Her voice was trembling.

I shut my eyes as tightly as I could and began praying, trying with everything I could muster to simply send my spirit into the arms of Jesus and escape this awful agony. And at some point—I'm not sure exactly when—I suddenly felt I actually could do it. That I could choose my moment of death and will myself into heaven. Was that a realistic feeling? Is the whole idea of willfully "releasing one's spirit" even feasible? I don't know. Honestly I'm skeptical about the whole thing now. But that was the way I felt at that moment.

No, I didn't see a bright light or a tunnel or anything like that, but—and here's the part you might disbelieve—behind the darkness of my eyelids I did see a doorway appear.[7]

Was it a vision of some sort? Or simply a hallucination? That's for you to decide; I'm just going to tell you what happened next. It was as if I were standing in an unlit anteroom and had discovered an opening into the next room. My sense was that all I had to do was walk through that door and I would accomplish my goal, that heaven awaited me across that threshold.

I desperately wanted to go through that door.

Before I could take one step toward it, the door suddenly opened from the other side. A figure appeared, filling the doorway and blocking my way. I didn't see his face or anything more than the shadow of him, but I knew without any doubt that Christ himself was standing there, preventing me from leaving.

I felt more than saw the frown on his face; and for the first and only time ever in my life, I heard his voice speak audibly to me: "It's not time yet."

I was devastated.

No, I was more than devastated, more than disconsolate. I can't even begin to explain to you the absolute desolation I felt at that moment, except to say that just remembering and writing it right now is causing tears of sorrow for me once again. Yes, I was unhappy about being denied entry into his glory. But what was worse to endure was the pure shame I felt at having tried to force my way in—and the heartbreak at having to hear disappointment in his voice.

"It's not time yet."

I heard those words, heard that voice, and suddenly I knew it was more awful to face my savior's slightest disappointment than to endure a thousand days of whatever my mystery illness was.

Now let me be clear: I wasn't fearful in the slightest about any possible punishment; there were no threats made nor any received. And why would there be? Christ already took the punishment for my sin; he knew it and I knew it. But I will tell you I was newly afraid of *disappointing* my awe-inducing Savior— more afraid of that than anything else I could dream of at that moment.

The vision disappeared and I immediately quit trying to "release my spirit." I heard my wife finishing up her phone conversation in the other room. And I started sobbing uncontrollably. I felt like a disobedient child who'd been reprimanded by a loving but firm parent, and that was worse than the pain of my illness. I never wanted to face him like that ever again.

My wife came back into the room and found me overwhelmed with grief. "He said I can't go yet," I sobbed. "He said I can't go." I don't know if she understood exactly what had just happened, but she seemed very relieved. "I'm glad," she said. "I'm so glad."

Now, I did eventually recover from that sickness, but I've never forgotten that meeting. My life, as I mentioned in previous chapters, has not been easy since then. Truth is, it's often been hard. I've often found myself in crazy storms—facing people who intended me harm and who sometimes succeed in causing it, facing new troubles that surprise and overwhelm me, facing the unhappy outcomes of my own sinful nature. I'm sometimes afraid for my future, for my family, for my country, for my career, for many, many things. But whenever some new *mĕgas sĕismós* spins my world out of control, I see in my mind's eye that doorway into mystery, and I remember the promise I've found to be true since then: "The LORD is my helper, so I will have no fear" (Hebrews 13:6 NLT).

Instead of terrifying me senseless, Jesus' frightening wonder is—slowly, day-by-day, in tiny little mustard-seed increments—becoming comfort and strength enough for me to face every new storm.

Two Choices When Life Spins Out of Control

It is both frightening and wonderful to experience the storms of life with Christ in the boat. And when that whirlwind inevitably happens, I've learned that you and I have two choices: (1) we can surrender *to* our circumstances, or (2) we can surrender *within* our circumstances.

We can let our circumstances define the way we live our lives, the way we respond, the way to act and react—and fail to achieve our hoped-for outcome more often than not anyway. Or within any circumstance we can look to Jesus, trusting him for help and guidance and letting him determine the outcome.

Sue Sawyer saw firsthand how that can work. In 1985, Sue worked as a nurse in an intensive care unit at a hospital. In that kind of environment, it would have been futile to say to her, "You worry about life too much. Relax and enjoy it." Sue couldn't do that.

Every day she was confronted with patients who were staring death in the face. If she wasn't thinking about it, they were. When they weren't thinking about death, they were reliving their lives and sharing their most private fears and feelings with her.

"I felt privileged to be the recipient of their reflections," she says now. "I knew that these World War II and Korean War vets were speaking words of wisdom. Some men had been at Normandy. They told of being in foxholes with guns blazing and bullets flying overhead. Some stories may have been embellished with time, but I didn't mind. That just made them more fascinating!"

Women often spoke of loved ones—spouses, children, and friends. All of them, men and women, were teaching Sue that there was more to life than just living.

Two individuals are etched on Sue's mind. One was an LOL—that's an acronym Sue and her colleagues used as an endearing term for "little old lady." This LOL was in Sue's unit just a short time.

One day the LOL clicked on her call light, and Sue was the only nurse available to respond. "You're not my patient today," Sue said. "Do you want me to get your nurse?" Sue knew how much LOLs liked to talk, and that day she was just too busy to listen. But the lady was insistent.

"No need for that," the LOL said. "I just wanted to tell you something. Now shut the door, honey."

Sue knew she was in for a long talk. *Arrgh*, she thought. *Oh well. I guess I can listen for a bit.* The lady took Sue's hand.

"I know I'm dying," she said. "I have waited my whole life to see Jesus, and now I will see him soon. I am so excited." She paused, patted Sue's hand, and then squeezed it. "That's all I want to say, honey."

Sue muttered, "Isn't that wonderful!" and left feeling puzzled and troubled.

A week or so later Sue witnessed a man's death. He was one of the World War II vets who had been a boxer in the air force.

"I stood outside his room and watched," Sue recalled. "As his blood pressure and heart rate began to decelerate, he started wildly swinging his arms in the air. He must have thought he was losing consciousness during a boxing match. The picture spoke so loudly, it was so symbolic. I stood transfixed, watching. The man was raging against the 'dying of the light.' He was so different from the lady I had talked to the previous week."

Sue went home that night deeply troubled by the boxer's death. She thought, *He was so different from the little old lady. I wonder which way I will face death—at peace, the way the little old lady did, or swinging wildly, fighting against the unknown, the way the boxer did.*

Life had gotten irretrievably out of control for both the LOL and the boxer. They each faced a *měgas sěismŏs* of imminent, unstoppable death. The boxer fought with all he had in him, but he had to fight alone, and it just wasn't enough. In the end, all he could do was surrender helplessly to his circumstances.

The little old lady faced the same fight, but with Jesus by her side. In the end, she chose to surrender herself completely to Christ *within* her fatal circumstance—and that became her everlasting victory.

Oh, and one other thing. A few days later Sue's friend Diane invited her over for spaghetti. The conversation turned to life, death, and eternity. With the memory of the LOL and the boxer fresh in her mind, Sue Sawyer chose that little old lady's way and committed her life to Jesus, for now and for forevermore.

"What a creative God," Sue says today. "He orchestrated my circumstances so perfectly that they collectively wooed me to him. I'm touched by the fact that he knew how to gently call me, a sinner, to come home."

Frightening Wonder

It is no safe thing to place yourself wholly into the care of one such as Christ. That's evident from the lives of his original disciples.

When the *měgas sěismŏs* erupted on the Sea of Galilee a few thousand years ago, it was entirely possible that God might have let them all drown. After all, only a few years later he let ten of the twelve be tortured and murdered. Of the other two, Judas betrayed Christ and killed himself; John was tortured and miraculously survived his intended execution.[8]

Additionally Christian history is filled with the suffering of the saints. A peek inside the walls of your church will reveal more of the same happening today. My guess is that you, too, have personally experienced pain while being held firmly in the hand of God.

But take heart, friend. When your life feels as if it's spinning dangerously out of control, when you are overcome with pain or sorrow or heartache or weakness or illness or unkindness or decay or self-loathing or bitterness or hollowness or grief or any other God-awful moment this sin-bloodied world so routinely serves us, Christ's Holy Spirit is not sleeping. He never does. We can call on his power anytime, anywhere, for any reason, and let his confidence rule the storms of life, no matter how hard the wind blows.

Does that mean Jesus will always calm your storms? That every problem you now face will be miraculously solved? That every operating-room scuffle you endure will end quickly, safely, and to your liking? You know the scary answer to those questions. But by now you also must know what the disciples learned after witnessing Jesus display his frightening power over nature itself: our Savior is awesome, terrible, and wonderful all at once.

Sometimes he will speak peace to the wind and still the storms of your life circumstances. Other times he will take you *through* the storm rather than *out* of it. He will speak comfort to your heart and let the storms rage on while you and he knit yourselves closer together for warmth and courage to face another day, another storm.

Either way, he is God, he is in control—and he is not sleeping.

FIVE

STOLEN MIRACLES

No man can steal what is already his.

—ANONYMOUS

The LORD is good to those who hope in him.

—LAMENTATIONS 3:25 NCV

N ot a single one of the gospel writers bothered to remember her name.

That seems careless at best, and not just a little unkind. After all, they knew and spoke freely about other very private details of her life. They even made the story of her encounter with Jesus a matter of public conversation, a shining testimony of faith and God's grace. But in all that preaching and teaching and testifying, nobody thought to offer her the simple dignity of mentioning her name. Go figure.

Bible historians from later centuries tell us that Mark, when creating his gospel account that includes this woman's story, "wrote down accurately all that Peter remembered of Jesus' words and works."[1] Peter was actually there when this woman encountered Christ, and he experienced her miracle. Peter probably even talked to her personally. How else would he have known the background info revealed in Mark 5:21–34? Yet when Peter told Mark about this woman, he apparently remembered everything except her name.[2]

Because of that apostolic oversight, history has mostly remembered our anonymous heroine with the unwieldy title of . . . ahem: Woman with an Issue of Blood.[3]

How's that for embarrassing?

This remarkable lady made a mark in history; she's known worldwide! That's the good news. The bad news is that she's been remembered through the ages as a woman with menstrual problems. How'd you like that for your eternal reputation? It just seems a little unfair. Still, for twelve years this nameless woman suffered from uterine bleeding; and yes, she was finally healed through a compassionate miracle of Christ.

As Mark records in chapter 5, verses 21 to 34, when Jesus once walked through Galilee, an anonymous woman was there, a woman whose monthly period had inexplicably, and almost unbearably, stretched on uninterrupted for 144 long months.

I imagine that in the press of the crowd she was nearly invisible, hiding in plain view, living underneath the line of sight of those who surrounded her. She was used to that by now. It felt comfortable. And, like everyone around her, she was caught up in this thrilling moment. Jesus of Nazareth *himself* was passing through her little corner of Galilee! She could see him, practically touch him, he was that close.

Out of the masses she saw a synagogue ruler emerge—yeah, the disciples remembered *his* name: Jairus. She heard Jairus asking the Messiah for something impossible. And almost without warning, an equally impossible plan began to form in her head. She was going to steal a miracle.

Everybody Wants Something

There is no bigger celebrity in history than Jesus Christ, and two thousand years ago that was just as obvious as it is today. One of the downsides of being a celebrity is that pretty much everybody wants something from you—and Jesus was no exception. Hollywood legend Dick Van Dyke told a story that gives a little glimpse of what that's like.

It seems Dick was headed to work one morning when his car seized up and died. Blue and gray smoke billowed out from under the hood of his Jaguar, and in seconds, the star of timeless films like *Mary Poppins* and *Chitty Chitty Bang Bang* found himself stranded in the middle lane of the freeway, during rush hour, in the rain. According to Dick, "That's when the real problems started."

He got out of his car and started waving to passing motorists in hopes that they'd make room so he could push his car out of traffic and onto the shoulder of the road. "People began to recognize me," he says. At first he was relieved when several motorists left their cars parked in traffic and came toward him. Then he found out why they hurried eagerly to his side: they wanted autographs.

After a moment, a guy named Tom appeared and exclaimed what a lucky break it was for Dick's car to have broken down. Tom was a film producer, and he had the perfect script for Mr. Van Dyke to read. He enthusiastically hand delivered it right there on the freeway, excited that *the* Dick Van Dyke might star in his movie.

Finally two police officers showed up to help—which they did eventually. But first they both just *had* to perform impromptu dance auditions for the stranded Hollywood star. Turns out, both cops were amateur dancers, and they hoped Dick would help them break into show business.

At last Dick and his car were towed to a local mechanic's

shop where his Jaguar could be repaired. Surprise! The owner of the shop was a former vaudeville player. Since Dick was a captive audience, he insisted on performing his vaudeville routine for the film celebrity in his midst while the car was being fixed.

In all, Mr. Van Dyke said drily, "It turned out to be an interesting morning."[4]

That's the cost of fame, I suppose. If that kind of ruckus can happen with Dick Van Dyke, you can imagine what it must have been like when news spread that Jesus, a bona fide miracle worker, was walking around in the streets of Galilee! It didn't take long for a large crowd to form around him, and the reason is obvious: everybody *wants something from God.*

We're remarkably self-centered creations, aren't we? If you don't believe it, listen to your prayers tonight. If they're like mine, they sound embarrassingly close to the humorous lyrics from Larry Bryant's song, "Shopping List": "Gimme this, I want that . . ."[5]

Yeah, that sounds about right.

We want God to do for us all those indulgent things we would do for ourselves if we could, and that's what we spend most of our time asking for. But those things are really just the surface of our desperate need. Thankfully, God sees past that fluff and down to the underneath stuff, to those things we're often embarrassed to admit even to ourselves.

The woman with the issue of blood was no exception. In the billowing crowd surrounding the Savior, she saw Jesus walking by, and she wanted healing. She wanted wholeness. She wanted—she needed—a demonstration of God's compassion for her, a touch of kindness from the only one who could give lasting relief from her pain.

But how to get that?

How do you push your way publicly into the presence of a religious superstar like Jesus and present him with your embarrassing, private ailment—especially when more prestigious people are already clamoring for his attention?

Well, if you can't ask for a miracle outright, maybe you look for a way to sneak one when nobody's looking. And that's what this woman decided to do.

What's crazy is that her little plan worked.

What a Girl Wants

"When Jesus had again crossed over by boat to the other side of the lake, a large crowd gathered around him . . . and pressed around him. And a woman was there who had been subject to bleeding for twelve years" (Mark 5:21, 24–25).

The woman with an issue of blood was probably in her mid- to late-twenties. According to one theologian, "[Her] ailment probably started after puberty; given an average life expectancy of about forty years and the 'twelve years' she had been ill, she may have spent half or all her adult life with this trouble."[6]

I'm told by one with authority in these matters—my wife—that enduring a monthly period is not terribly pleasant. Oh you get used to it, of course, but I don't know any woman who actually looks forward to it. To experience uterine bleeding once a month is trouble enough for most women; to experience it all month, every month, for months on end must have been physically and emotionally exhausting. And yet that physical bleeding was not the worst of this woman's afflictions.

By nearly every measure, the woman with an issue of blood lived her life in the underneath spaces of her world. Her closest contemporary cousin would be a person from a Dalit (untouchable) caste in India. By virtue of her feminine discharge, she was literally shunned by everyone in her society.[7] This was not simply a community prejudice; it was required by God himself and recorded by Moses in Leviticus 15.

Why would God command this kind of treatment for a physical process he himself created? I've heard some speculate that it was part of Eve's punishment from the garden of Eden. I've heard others suggest that due to the generally unsanitary practices of ancient peoples, this command was mostly rooted in God's concern for human health and well-being. But the real answer is, I don't know. What I do know is that according to Jewish law and customs at the time, the woman with an issue of blood was

- considered unclean, both physically and spiritually;
- to be confined to her home while menstruating—which, for her, was all the time;
- not allowed to touch *anybody*. Her family members weren't even allowed to lie on a bed or sit on a chair that she had touched.

Her family, her friends (if she had any), her neighbors, her religious leaders, her political leaders—they all viewed her as somehow polluted by her menstrual function. People who touched her even by accident were considered contaminated right alongside her and had to (a) take a bath to purify themselves; (b) wash their clothes; and (c) stay isolated until evening. She was forced away from religious gatherings, from temple worship, from even joyous annual religious feasts that consumed her culture in regular intervals.[8]

Even Gentile cultures of that time had similar rules in this regard. For instance, the Roman philosopher Pliny dictated that the touch of a menstruating woman was invisibly harmful and to be avoided. Some extremists forbade even speaking with a menstruating woman or making eye contact with her because her breath was poisonous and her gaze was injurious.[9]

Can you imagine the absolute isolation this woman must have felt? The emotional longing that overlaid her physical suffering? I believe you can; I suspect we all can. Let me share a behind-the-scenes story from the hit Broadway show *Wicked* to explain why.

In case you're unfamiliar with it, *Wicked* is a lavish musical that imagines what might have happened in life to turn Elphaba—a talented, green-skinned young woman (originally portrayed magnificently by Idina Menzel)—into the Wicked Witch of the West from the land of Oz. It's much fun. At any rate, when the soundtrack to this show released in December 2003, author Gregory Maguire, who wrote the novel on which *Wicked* is based, and several cast members attended a party to celebrate that event in the lobby of the Gershwin theatre.

I'll let Gregory tell you what happened next:

> I just sat on the stairs and watched a line of four or five hundred people slowly snaking along. Every fourteenth person or so getting their CD signed was a young woman between the ages of about 15 and 25. And many of them were women of color. There were a lot of Asian women and some Pakistani women wearing headscarves. Many of them just burst into tears. And

Idina [Menzel] kept getting out of her chair and leaning over the table awkwardly and hugging these young women, who looked at her and said, "You're the first person to demonstrate how I feel in my own life, how alone I feel, and how much I long to be empowered."[10]

If you've ever felt like those young women in line at the *Wicked* CD release party—and who hasn't?—then you, too, have an inkling of what the woman with an issue of blood must have felt, what she experienced, what she longed for.

If you've ever lived that kind of silent desperation, tried to blink it away in the first light of morning, hidden its cries in muffled sobs of midnight, smelled it on the breath exhaled from your very own mouth, then you know what she wanted, what she needed.

Yes, the woman with an issue of blood wanted physical healing, that's true. But I think she needed more than just that. What she needed most was what would come *after* the healing:

Restoration

Acceptance

Affection

Compassion

Belonging

Love

Crime of Compassion

In my mind's eye, she is hunched over, wearing an expression that crosses between resignation and expectation. She keeps out of the way but also manages to stay agonizingly close at all times, slipping through the crowd in shadows and small openings, waiting, listening—present, but rarely seen.

People are all around her, pushing and swaying, flowing. In a way, it's a little intoxicating to be swept up in this mass of humanity, to feel the heat of human bodies all around, even to smell the sweat of men who barely notice her, who are unaware of her tainting effect on them. If they knew her secret, their fury would surely be immediate and fierce. But today they, like her, are focused on something else, drawn like a tidal wave toward the man in the middle of it all.

Jesus of Nazareth is walking down the road. *So close . . .*

So many people. So many disciples. But only one woman with a terrible secret, a hidden hope, and a desperate plan.

That kind of desperation must have been what drove her to first seek cures from the supposed doctors and professional healers of her time. Ever wonder what kind of treatments they offered? The Babylonian Talmud shared a list of procedures for curing this woman's condition that she likely endured. Here is my summary of just a few:

- Eat barley grain taken from the dung of a white mule, then try not to have a bowel movement for three days.
- Sit at a crossroads, holding a cup of wine, until a man comes up from behind and scares you by shouting, "Cease your discharge!"
- Have your doctor smear sixty pieces of clay on you— presumably around your vaginal area—while saying to you, "Cease your discharge!"
- Boil fenugreek, saffron, and cumin in wine, then drink

it while your doctor inanely commands, "Cease your discharge!"[11]

I could go on, but you get the point.

It's that kind of life experience that we see painted on this woman's face as she's sneaking through the crowd around Christ. And it's that kind of desperation that motivates her to attempt the unthinkable, to dare to pickpocket a healing from the hem of Rabbi Jesus' garment.

Honestly, do you blame her?

Now, I've heard preachers expound on Mark 5:21–34, saying that the woman with an issue of blood premeditated this heavenly heist, that she'd heard countless stories of Jesus' previous miracles and thus preplanned her strategy for receiving her own miracle from him. I suppose that view could be true, but I have trouble buying it. It seems to mistake the chronology of events as they're related in this passage, and doesn't take into account the impulsive force of her act.

Mark 5:21 sets the scene by telling us there was a large crowd surrounding Jesus. Then in verse 25 Scripture reveals that our heroine has already been skulking about in that crowd. Verse 27 continues, "When she heard about Jesus, she came up behind him in the crowd and touched his cloak."

To my view, that sounds more like a crime of passion than one of premeditation. When she *heard*, she *acted*. How did she hear?

It's interesting to note that this story in Mark 5 is actually two stories. I've often wondered why the miracle of Jairus and his daughter was framed around the miracle of the woman with an issue of blood. After studying it awhile, that one phrase in verse 27 explains it for me: "When she heard . . ."

She was in the crowd—the social outcast—watching, listening. Then came Jairus—respected and admired by society—accosting Jesus and begging mercy for his daughter with these words: "Please come and put your hands on her so that she will be healed and live" (Mark 5:23).

And, in my opinion, that's when the lightbulb lit up in this woman's mind. In Jairus's plea she'd just heard firsthand of Jesus' healing power—and saw a respected, credible leader placing his unquestioned faith in that power. It's not a long leap to imagine her thinking at that moment, *Jesus can heal—Jairus said so! And if his touch can heal that dying girl, then it can also heal a bleeding woman.*

"When she heard about Jesus," Mark's gospel tells us, "she came up behind him in the crowd and touched his cloak, because she thought, 'If I just touch his clothes, I will be healed'" (5:27–28).

Crime of passion.

Healing of compassion.

She heard Jairus's testimony. She believed it. She reached out in faith to take it for herself. And the unthinkable happened. After twelve long, heartbreaking, debilitating, agonizing years, the unthinkable finally happened.

And he let her steal a miracle.

How cool is that?

Compassion Is Christ's Nature

At the exact moment she touched Jesus' cloak, the woman with an issue of blood instantly became the woman healed from an issue of blood. The crazy part of this story is not that she was healed, but that Jesus appears to have healed her without even trying.

There are many theories about how that could happen, some involving Trinity theology, some involving voluntary incarnational limitation, some suggesting secret Christological schemes, and so on. Those are all well and good, and may even be true, but one fact remains: the woman healed from an issue of blood took her miracle without asking Christ's permission.

So why did he give it to her? Let me add my simple theory to the mix: compassion is Christ's nature.

Fire naturally burns hot. Birds naturally grow feathers. A rose naturally emits a rosy fragrance. And God naturally expresses compassion. This is, after all, how God described himself.

Remember when he appeared before Moses? God passed before the prophet and called out his own name, saying:

> *Yahweh! The LORD!*
> *The God of compassion and mercy!*
> *I am slow to anger*
> *and filled with unfailing love and faithfulness.*
> *I lavish unfailing love to a thousand generations.*
> (Exodus 34:6–7 NLT)

Do you grasp the significance of an infinite, unlimited God declaring that he is "the God of compassion," that he is "filled" with unfailing love? In a way that's more real than we can ever dream or understand, God's love *fills* his infinite being with limitless capacity for compassion. That simply boggles the mind.

What's more, if the gospel writers are telling the truth—and I believe they are!—Jesus' compassionate nature was the catalyst for a number of healings and miracles, including healings of all kinds of sicknesses, the feeding of the four thousand, healing the blind, cleansing lepers, and even raising the dead.[12]

Theologians John Walvoord and Roy Zuck point out one last interesting tidbit in this regard. When expositing on Mark's phrase in 5:30, "At once Jesus realized that power had gone out from him," they share this as the literal interpretation of that Greek text: Jesus knew fully that "power from Him (on account of who He is) had gone out."[13]

Christ was miraculously compassionate toward the woman with an issue of blood because *that's just who he is.* She attempted to steal a miracle, but in reality all she did was embrace what was already hers. His inherent, limitless compassion made it something that was already hers for the taking.

Does that mean that any miracle you or I desire awaits our casual attempt to get it? Don't be silly. There is one last thing we must learn from the experience of the woman healed from an issue of blood:

Christ's Compassion Is Bigger Than Your Vision

Remember what I said earlier about our heroine? She desperately wanted healing, but she desperately *needed* what that healing would bring. She needed restoration and acceptance. She needed affection and compassion. She needed to belong. She needed love. And after her menstrual functions had been restored to health, Jesus refused to let her leave until she got it all.

Do you understand what this means for you and me today? Christ, in his great compassion, will sometimes force his vision of what you and I need and, in the process, overrule our own visions of miracles we think we want. You see, compassion isn't just sympathy—though it certainly includes that element. True compassion is *strength that's shared*; it's God's *agápē* love acted out on behalf of the object of his love—you. Sometimes that means Christ's compassion won't allow you to take the easy way out as he works toward making your life better.

"Wait a minute, Mike," I hear you saying. "She was healed! She got exactly what she wanted."

Well, did she get exactly what she wanted? Take a closer look at what happened next.

> At once Jesus realized that power had gone out from him. He turned around in the crowd and asked, "Who touched my clothes?" . . . Jesus kept looking around to see who had done it. Then the woman, knowing what had happened to her, came and fell at his feet and, trembling with fear, told him the whole truth. (Mark 5:30, 32–33)

Now, imagine you are the woman who has just stolen yourself a miracle. What do you want most in the world at that moment? To get away scot-free, of course! To go home unnoticed and avoid any anger from the people in the crowd. After all, you've just contaminated everyone around you—you've even placed your polluting hand on Rabbi Jesus. If he knew you'd touched him and made him unclean, wouldn't he curse you and cast you away? If the others knew you'd defiled them *and* the Son of God, wouldn't their hatred and disgust lead them to act violently toward you? Of course it would. You've spent the last twelve years learning that hard lesson.

But then, right after the best possible thing you can imagine has happened to you, the worst possible thing you can imagine is about to happen.

Jesus demands to know *who touched him*. Being exposed could cost her life!

Despite his disciples' sarcastic grumbling in Mark 5:31, he refuses to stop searching for the person who touched him—for *you*.

Scripture tells us Jesus "kept looking"—which indicates she kept hiding! Despite her healing, do you think she felt good at that moment? Do you think she appreciated Jesus intentionally and doggedly putting her on the spot like that? Demanding her public humiliation? Putting her safety and quite possibly her life in danger?

Doubtful.

Truth is, she was terrified by Jesus' relentless pursuit. She was literally shaking with fear (see verse 33). She had just been healed; she should have been dancing for joy. Instead she feared for her life. How awful would that be?

Finally she gave up her own plans—her escape—and surrendered herself to Christ's awful, insistent demands. She came forward. She fell at his feet. She confessed it all. And then, instead of anger or reprimand or call for retribution, she got so much more than she wanted; she got everything she desperately needed.

"Daughter," Jesus said to her, "your faith has healed you. Go in peace and be freed from your suffering" (Mark 5:34). In those fifteen little words, Jesus had given her restoration, acceptance, affection, compassion, belonging, *love*.

And he did it *publicly*!

By divine example, he had just commanded anyone within

hearing distance—and everyone who would hear of it later—to accept the woman healed from an issue of blood in peace and freedom, as a treasured member of his own holy family.

By divine decree, he declared that she was to be restored to full relationship and privilege within their world. No longer was she allowed to suffer isolation and degradation and abuse; she was his daughter, his family. She *belonged*.

By divine endorsement, he even gave her new, prestigious societal status as an example of pure faith to everyone around her. According to theologian Craig Keener, "Given the frequent failure of the male disciples' faith, Mark's record of this woman's faith is all the more striking."[14]

None of that would have happened if she'd been successful with a smash-and-grab healing; if Jesus had healed her and then allowed her to run away unseen. If she'd escaped from the full impact of Christ's compassion toward her, she'd have missed her true miracle.

Was it pleasant for this woman to endure public confession? To face possible retaliation and violence at the hands of the crowd? Of course not. But that hardship was necessary to fulfill Jesus' compassionate vision for his daughter of faith.

So, let me ask you again: Do you understand what this means for you and me today? Christ, in his great compassion, will sometimes force his vision of what you and I need and, in the process, overrule our own visions of miracles we think we want.

Our job is not to demand of God a certain kind of miracle that fits neatly with our own ambitions: *Heal me, Lord! Fix my finances, Lord! Move me to a new home, Lord! Punish my enemies, Lord! Make my book a bestseller, Lord! Don't let me fail at this job, Lord! Take me out of this circumstance, Lord!* God sympathizes with all those problems—but in his great compassion, those hardships can be orchestrated to bring about the greater miracle in your life.

Our job is not to define God's compassion in miracles or specific blessings or healings. Our job is to trust fully in the complete working of his compassion in our lives—when we like it and when we don't like it. To trust God's compassion when it delivers inexpressible joy and when it scares us to the point of trembling. To trust God when it means we must be exposed to uncomfortable seasons and circumstances. And to trust Jesus even when his vision for us appears to be radically different from our expectations of him.

Aesop once said, "If men had all they wished, they would often be ruined," and he's right.[15] Thanks be to God that he's so much more than a miracle machine! His compassion is so much bigger than my vision. The woman healed from an issue of blood learned that truth the hard way, and now, thanks to her great example, we can learn anew each day.

SIX

TATTERED FAITH

*Faith isn't pretending our problems don't exist, nor
is it simply blind optimism. Faith points us beyond
our problems to the hope we have in Christ.*

—BILLY GRAHAM[1]

Now faith is the substance of things hoped for.

—HEBREWS 11:1 NKJV

f you knew that—today only—God would answer one question of yours, what would you ask?"

During the summer of 2012, I posed that survey question to Christian teenagers and their youth leaders from all across the nation. It was billed as a "spontaneous question for God," but judging by the responses, these kids were already peppering God with questions—and hungry for his answers. I'd hoped to get about eight hundred teens to participate in this study. In the end, roughly two thousand submitted their questions for God! A sampling:

"What do you look like?"

"Why all the fear and judgment by many who claim your name?"

"Will I see my dad in heaven?"

"God, why is it so hard for me to be happy?"

"Why . . . why everything?"

These questions—and the 1,995 others I collected—reveal a simple truth about humanity: everybody has a question for God.

Some of our questions are ordinary. "What'll I have for breakfast this morning?" Some are philosophical. "Why all the fear and judgment by your followers?" Some are theoretical in nature. "What does God look like?" But there are a sacred few that present matters of life and death and eternity—and it's those questions that plague us in the dark moments, in the times when we're alone, and uncertain, and feeling our faith shrink away in confusion and fear.

For Jesus' cousin John the Baptist, it was that kind of question that haunted his thoughts while he languished as a political prisoner in the cold, stone prison of Machaerus. And when he was given the opportunity to ask one question he knew God would answer, he didn't hesitate.

A Question of Faith

"Are you the one who is to come, or should we expect someone else?" (Matthew 11:3).

What a great question—especially when you consider that John the Baptist was the one who asked it of Jesus.

John splashed onto the scene near the beginning of Jesus' public ministry. To say the baptizer was odd would be an understatement; he could reasonably be called Jesus' eccentric, homeless cousin. John lived, monklike, in the desert of Judea, where he deliberately shunned most of the expected conventions of his modern culture. For instance, this wild man dressed in clothes made of camel hair and survived mostly on a diet of locusts and wild honey.[2]

Nonetheless, he was a confidant of God himself.

Luke 3:2 reports that "the word of God came to John . . . in the wilderness." From that moment on, the nutty guy in the desert was the sanest person in Israel. He started preaching, there in the wastelands, and crowds flocked to him. Inexplicably, he became something of a celebrity, attracting a number of disciples and finding attentive crowds wherever he went. He essentially had rock-star status.

John's message to the adoring crowds was always the same: repent and be baptized as a sign of that repentance; live an honest, righteous lifestyle; and await the soon coming of God's Messiah (Luke 3:1–18).

During this time, John had at least one otherworldly experience: he baptized Jesus in the river Jordan. At the moment when he raised Christ from the water, John said, "I saw the Spirit come down from heaven as a dove and remain on him. . . . I have seen and I testify that this is the God's Chosen One" (John 1:32, 34).

Pretty heady stuff, huh? John had seen with his own eyes that his cousin Jesus was the hoped-for, promised Messiah; the full incarnation of eternity; the one and only Son of God! And then . . .

Time passed.

Followers came and went.

King Herod Antipas, also known as Herod the tetrarch, committed public sins of marital corruption, and John the Baptist began to call him out for it. Because of John's popularity and influence, the king took a frowning notice. Rather than let this noisy preacher continue to rail against him publicly, Antipas exacted his vengeance. He dumped John in a prison cell, locking him up indefinitely in the castle fortress of Machaerus, located just east of the Dead Sea in Judea.[3]

Can you imagine what a small, square, stone room like that would do to a man like John? He had been free—truly *free*—out there in the wilderness. The sky and the land were open before him at all times; his only restraint had been his own self-determination. He was a man beautifully at home in the great open spaces of the Judean desert, now locked like a bird in a cage, trapped in darkness, trotted out as a prize and conversation piece from time to time, but mostly left alone and confined, waiting for the day when Herod would finally tire of his toy and send an executioner with a sword to end his life.

Although we don't know exactly what John's prison cell in Machaerus was like, we can make a reasonable guess about this kind of "Roman hospitality" based on the Tullianum prison in the center of the city of Rome, where Simon Peter would later be jailed. The only prison in Rome proper, it was "a conical, windowless chamber of rough-hewn tufa, the only entrance to which is a hole in the floor of the room above."[4] According to historians, "Prisoners were flung through this hole into the prison, and on occasion left there to starve and rot."[5] A Numidian king named Jugurtha was imprisoned there in 104 BC, and his first comment was that it was unbearably cold down there. Sallust, a Roman politician and historian from the generation before Christ, described Tullianum this way: "Repulsive and terrible on account of neglect, dampness and smell."[6]

In Machaerus, it's likely that John's prison cell was comparable to Tullianum—and the Baptist suffered more than a year imprisoned in these kinds of conditions.[7] Can you imagine the physical and emotional agony in that cell? I can, and I don't like it. Just thinking about it makes me feel a little claustrophobic.

In a situation like John's, faith might fray at the edges, resolve might begin to tatter and unmake itself in your mind and heart. And here's something I've noticed that I'm sure John realized and perhaps you can relate to: sometimes in the darkness it's hard to believe what you saw clearly in the light.

Abraham Lincoln knew something of this kind of fraying darkness in the days of despair he faced as president during the American Civil War. A scan through his public statements reveals this happening before our eyes. Consider, at the start of the War between the States, Lincoln was resolute and visionary. "The mystic chords of memory," he announced in his inaugural address on March 4, 1861, "stretching from every battlefield and patriot grave, to every living heart and hearthstone, all over this broad land, will yet swell the chorus of the Union."[8]

A little over a year into the war, on June 28, 1862, his rhetoric was tempered but still firm and uncompromising: "I expect to maintain this contest until successful, or till I die, or am conquered."[9]

And then the true darkness began to fall. After a devastating defeat at Manassas in Virginia, Lincoln began first to worry, and then to doubt his cause: "Well, we are whipped again, I am afraid," he moaned. "What shall we do? The bottom is out of the tub, the bottom is out of the tub!" (August, 1862).[10]

The next months and years for Lincoln were lived in near-constant, faith-shaking darkness and despair:

"If there is a worse place than Hell, I am in it."
(DECEMBER 1862, AFTER DEFEAT AT FREDERICKSBURG)[11]

"My God! My God! What will the country say?"
(MAY 1863, AFTER DEFEAT AT CHANCELLORSVILLE)[12]

"This war is eating my life out. I have a strong impression that I shall not live to see the end."

(1864)[13]

And then, in the deep darkness a flicker of hope burst into flame.

Union victories began turning the tide of the Civil War, and we can see Lincoln's confidence beginning to recover. Once again his rhetoric begins to soar, to reach resolutely toward his vision of one United States of America. In March 1865, about a month before Lee's surrender, Lincoln is able to regather his faith and speak these eloquent words: "With malice toward none; with charity for all; with firmness in the right [as God gives], let us strive on to finish the work we are in; to bind up the nation's wounds . . . to do all which may achieve a just, and a lasting peace" (Second Inaugural Address, March 4, 1865).[14]

And finally, less than two weeks before his death, President Lincoln proclaimed the end of his trials: "Thank God I have lived to see this. It seems to me that I have been dreaming a horrid dream for four years, and now the nightmare is gone" (April 3, 1865).[15]

Gasping for life in the forgotten depths of his prison cell in Machaerus, John the Baptist must have experienced a journey of faith-shaking darkness and despair similar to what Abraham Lincoln endured. I'm deeply saddened by the suffering that John endured, but I'm also eternally grateful, because through example I've learned a very important truth about the life of faith and about faith in life:

Faith Is Often Different from Expectation

John the Baptist was, in some ways, a victim of his own mistaken expectations. Jews of his time—John included—expected a kick-butt Messiah, a political and military leader who would rain judgment down on enemies of righteousness. John himself had preached that the Messiah's "winnowing fork is in his hand to clear his threshing floor and to gather the wheat into his barn, but he will burn up the chaff with unquenchable fire" (Luke 3:17). John's faith in the Messiah was defined by his expectation of God's judgment on evildoers—especially folks like Herod Antipas and all his minions.

But Jesus didn't fit those expectations, and meanwhile John sat decaying in prison waiting for Christ to wreak his wrath.

Theologian George A. Buttrick explains John's predicament this way: "The waiting fretted his soul. . . . Doubt grew chiefly on the fact that Christ did not fulfill either the hope of the Messiah as nationalistically interpreted, or the picture that John himself had drawn."[16]

I suspect that there in the prison of Machaerus, John's great hope in Jesus at first remained strong, much like Lincoln's soaring vision of unity at the start of the Civil War. Then, as time passed, John's expectations slowly gave way to worry. *Where is Jesus? Why has he not brought God's judgment down on Herod and those like him?* And then that worry slipped into doubt. *Does Jesus not care? Was I wrong? Is Jesus not the Christ after all?*

At that point, John had two choices: (1) confront his doubts head-on and see if they had any merit or (2) surrender to his doubts and let them galvanize into despair.

When he heard that Jesus was nearby, he sent his disciples to ask of Christ himself: "Are you the one who is to come, or should we expect someone else?" (Matthew 11:3).

What a great question.

I so admire John the Baptist for having the guts to ask that, knowing where he was, knowing his own reputation, knowing his own very public previous testimony about Jesus!

John's faith was in tatters at this moment, and he needed to know the truth just to endure another day in Herod's prison cell, just to keep hope in the face of extreme hardship and sorrow. So he asked the tough question, the one that openly betrayed his doubts and fears and even threatened to undermine his own reputation and ministry.

Why did he ask this question? Legendary preacher John Wesley apparently didn't believe that a hero of faith like John the Baptist would ever have real doubts like this. So Wesley explained away John's tattered faith as merely a manipulative teaching opportunity. John sent his disciples to ask this question of Christ, Wesley decided, "not because he doubted himself; but to confirm their faith."[17]

Huh. Well, I suppose that contrived explanation *could* be true; after all, John Wesley has been right on many other counts.

But you know what I think? I think John wanted to know if Jesus was the one who was to come.

Look, sometimes when faith is frail, when darkness surrounds, when confidence is shaken and worry crosses over into the realm of doubt, you just have to ask the tough questions—even if your name is John the Baptist. And if God is the one from whom you need the answers, then he's the one you go to with your questions.

You know those sighing moments when words almost fail, when you've launched yourself uncompromisingly toward what you thought was God's will, only to find nothing but hardship and failure—and perhaps real danger—in that way. You've paused and looked up and asked, *Lord, is this you or not? Because if it's not, I want to get away from here.*

We all have these little crises of thinking. Fact is, I had one already this morning. And yesterday. And the day before. And underneath fortress Machaerus, cast away in a cruel prison cell, John's thought process also reached that kind of crisis point. He wanted to know—needed to know—that he wasn't making an intellectual, factual mistake about Jesus, that he wasn't rotting in prison while trusting in a flimsy case of mistaken identity.

"Are you the one who is to come?" Was Jesus indeed the fulfillment of messianic prophecies such as Psalm 118:26 and Zechariah 9:9?

The Case for Faith

It's interesting that John asked an academic question and Jesus responded with a legal answer. John's question really only required a yes-or-no reply, but instead of giving that simple solution, Jesus convened an impromptu, informal court—right there in front of God and everybody. Figuratively speaking, to answer John's great question, Christ took off the cloak of a rabbi and put on judicial robes instead.

"Go back," he instructed the Baptist's disciples, "and report to John what you hear and see."

> Exhibit A: "the blind receive sight,"
> Exhibit B: "the lame walk,"
> Exhibit C: "those who have leprosy are cleansed,"
> Exhibit D: "the deaf hear,"
> Exhibit E: "the dead are raised,"
> Exhibit F: "the good news is proclaimed to the poor."
> (Matthew 11:4–5).

Anyone familiar with Old Testament prophesies of Isaiah—and John was—would recognize fairly quickly that each and every one of these miracles was overwhelming proof of the promised Messiah, the Coming One.[18] In this way Jesus conclusively and forcefully answered John's faith crisis by placing the Baptist squarely in the jury box and saying essentially, "Look at the evidence, Cousin. You'll find the truth in there."

Why did Jesus do that?

Why did Jesus change the parameters of John's simple question into something of a courtroom drama? The author of Hebrews gives us a clue: "Faith," he said, "is the *substance* of things hoped for, the *evidence* of things not seen" (11:1 NKJV, emphasis added).

John the Baptist was having a crisis of faith.

John needed more than hope; he needed the *substance* of hope.

John needed more than a simple assent regarding what he couldn't see; he needed *evidence* of those unseen things.

No, it probably wasn't what John expected, but it was everything John needed. Jesus gave John substance on which to pin his hope and clear evidence to believe. In doing so, he gave John the gift of real, unshakable faith—faith that could carry him through any circumstance, faith that would endure in the depths of prison, faith that would remain strong even when the executioner came to bring a savage end to John's earthly life.

Faith Is *Not* Hope

Authentic faith, to those who do not or cannot see the true nature of life, must seem meaningless and empty, like a child's imaginary friend or a coin tossed in a wishing well. But authentic faith, to those who can grasp the nature of truth and apply it to life, is more than imagination or unseen potential. It is substance; it is reality; it is that which *is*, but which is also unseen.

Problem is, many Christians, myself included, have misunderstood faith to mean "hope" instead of the *substance* of hope. We're like Linus from the classic Peanuts cartoons, sermonizing to Charlie Brown about the fictional Great Pumpkin.

"On Halloween night," Linus fervently preaches, "the 'Great Pumpkin' rises up out of the pumpkin patch . . . and he brings toys to all the good little children in the world!"

When Charlie Brown tries to object, Linus keeps his faith (hope). "All right," he says, "so you believe in Santa Claus, and I'll believe in the 'Great Pumpkin.' The way I see it, it doesn't matter what you believe just so you're sincere."

And finally, November rolls around and this conversation takes place:

CHARLIE BROWN: "Well, Halloween has come and gone . . ."

LINUS: "So it has."

CHARLIE BROWN: "Did the 'Great Pumpkin' bring you lots of nice presents?"

LINUS (sulking): "Shut up!"[19]

Poor Linus! He confused the sincerity of hope with the true nature of faith, and the end result was disastrous. We chuckle at his error of belief, but let's face it: you and I are often guilty of doing the same.

No, we don't wait for some Great Pumpkin to appear at the

punkin' patch passing out loads of presents. But we are guilty of using the words *faith* and *hope* interchangeably, and then assuming with all sincerity that God will suddenly appear with loads of miracles, tailored just to our specifications, ready to grant our every wish.

That seemingly slight mix-up of thinking in regard to faith can be devastating. It changes the application of faith in life completely. Instead of saying, "I *know* this is true, and therefore will act on that truth," it causes a believer to say, "I hope this is true, and therefore I will gamble that my sincere hope will convince God to grant my request." That kind of faith/hope gamble is an injustice toward God and a disservice to you.

Pastor Chuck Swindoll has seen firsthand the tragic fallout from this mistaken approach to faith. He says:

> In thirty-eight years of ministry I have met thousands of people who hurt, their pain caused by every conceivable source. The most disillusioned among them anticipated but did not enjoy quick recovery.
>
> Many of these hurting folks were promised a "miracle"— but when no divine intervention transpired as advertised, their anguish reached the breaking point. I have looked into their faces and heard their cries. I have witnessed their response—everything from quiet disappointment to bitter, cursing cynicism . . . from tearful sadness to violent acts of suicide. Most have been sincere, intelligent, Christian people.[20]

That's what happens when we arrogantly substitute our limited hopes for God's limitless blessings of faith. If the experience of John the Baptist in Machaerus reveals any truth, if Hebrews 11:1

teaches us anything, it is this: it is not hope that gives rise to faith, but faith that gives rise to hope.

We do not *hope* and then exercise faith to bring that hope into being. We properly discern the truth—the substance of hope—in any given circumstance, then act in faith in ways that accord with the truth we have discerned. I call this the twofold test of faith, and when I find myself in need of a faith-filled reaction to the brass-knuckle experiences of life, I pause and ask myself the following two questions:

1. What is the truth (the substance) in this situation?
2. What is my best response—my act of faith—to that truth?

For instance, if I were to stand at the crossing of a railroad track and hear the whistle of a locomotive bearing down on me, I might be in a "moment of faith." So I'd ask the questions.

What is the truth of this situation? Well, the truth is that the train is speeding down the track. At that speed and this proximity, it would be unable to stop before this crossing and would likely crush under its metal hull anything standing on the track at this moment.

What is my best response to this locomotive truth? Understanding the potential danger—and the physics of collision—my best response would be to move away from the crossing and wait until the train has passed before I walk over to the other side. That, then, becomes my act of faith: moving away from danger and then waiting for the signal to come that tells me it is safe to pass.

And that's the way true faith can work in life's craziest situations. When hardship comes—and it does come!—you and I must discern God's truth and then move—or wait, or both—in response to that truth.

Often that will mean that we act in accordance with an unseen spiritual truth that may even be at odds with the perception of temporal reality—but that act of faith is never dangling, unsupported wishful thinking based on halfhearted hope or half-baked theology! It's based on eternal reality, on the *substance* of hope, and thus can elicit the confidence of complete trust in Jesus Christ to work through the existing situations of our lives.

Faith is not hope—faith is the substance of hope, the origin of hope. It is the truth upon which our hope can stand firm and unshaken, and that can therefore be trusted with our attitudes and actions. Therein lies our hope.

Faith Belongs in the Miracle Worker, Not in the Miracle

Look, I know God works miracles in the lives of his people. I've seen it happen in my own life and in my church. I've heard more stories than I can remember of intimate, supernatural ways God has intervened in the lives of Christians.

At this moment a literal flood of testimonies about this kind of faith is filling my brain! There's the one Phil Vischer told me during an interview about the beginnings of VeggieTales. There's the time when a bunch of college students found themselves unexpectedly at an exorcism. Or the story Andraé Crouch told me, also during an interview, about God's miraculous healing of Pastor Crouch's cancer. Or the timely provision of finances, the blessings of faithful friends, the whispers of Christ's love and his fingerprints in my life, and—oh!—so much more than I can ever write about.

But . . .

I also know that sometimes—actually, most often—God doesn't work big miracles in the daily lives of his followers.

Did you notice the miracle *not* happening in all the fuss of Matthew 11:1–6? John's disciples asked Jesus if he was indeed the hoped-for Messiah. Jesus responded with miraculous, incontrovertible evidence that fairly shouted, *"Yes!* The blind see! The deaf hear! The *dead* are raised!" Miracles abound, dripping freely from Christ almost like sweat on a workman's brow.

And yet there is no miracle for John the Baptist.

In later days, Simon Peter would find himself in prison, and an angel of God would appear to miraculously break that apostle out of jail (Acts 12:1–18). Paul and Silas would also be jailed, and before a single night could pass, Christ would send an earthquake to tear apart their prison and set them free (Acts 16:16–40).

Why didn't Jesus do something similar for John the Baptist?

We know that Christ held his cousin in high esteem. "Among those born of women," he said, "there has not risen anyone greater than John the Baptist" (Matthew 11:11). Yet Jesus left him to suffer, to languish alone in a rotting prison cell until the day he was murdered by an evil king.

Jesus didn't say to John, "Look at these miracles; they prove I am Christ! Now, get up in your prison cell, claim your own miracle, and be free. Rebuke your circumstances, and live up to your full potential as my follower. I've worked countless miracles in the lives of others, so that means you're entitled to on-demand miraculous treatment from me as well! Announce your miracle, and watch your chains fall away right now!"

We cannot presume upon our God's power. But that presumption sounds remarkably, distressingly familiar.

Yes, sometimes Christ will work miracles in the lives of his followers—and that's wonderful. But it doesn't mean that you and I are *entitled* to any miracle, given upon our command. It is no sin to ask Christ for help, even for a miracle. Honestly, it's a privilege of the family relationship we have with God. But it is sin to demand that God work miracles in your life as fulfillment of your current wish or expectation, and then to accuse him of faithlessness when he, in his infinite wisdom, chooses to lavish his love on you in ways that are different from your demand. Take heart—and maturity—from the experience of John the Baptist. Jesus bolstered John's faith—and then left him to suffer, knowing John's renewed confidence would be strong enough to endure.

Christians suffer setbacks and sorrows. That's not news to you. Christians pray and nothing happens. Loved ones die. Relationships crumble. Christians are persecuted and harmed at the hands of violent people.

When those things happen, some call out in supposed faith and say, "I believe *this* about God, therefore I expect *that* for myself." And when "that" doesn't happen, it shakes the faith of anyone involved. Others, in moments of hardship, have learned to say in authentic faith, "I know God to be faithful and true; therefore whatever happens to me can never change what I know is true."

The difference here is faith that's centered on a miracle and faith that's centered on the miracle worker. It's an issue of intimacy with and subsequent expectations for Jesus Christ. For instance . . .

The first believer operates in a miracle-centered faith that says something like, "I believe God heals, therefore I expect that God will heal me." If that healing doesn't come, this kind of faith is shaken. It immediately looks to place blame: "I didn't believe strong enough." "There's sin in my life." "I have angered God." That road leads only to heartache and legalism and untruth.

The second believer operates out of faith centered on the miracle worker, and therefore says, "I know Jesus loves me. Therefore, in either sickness or in health, I will experience God's love." This kind of faith may tire at times, it may fray a bit around the edges, but it can never truly be shaken.

Christ alone is the *substance* of our hope, the truth on which we rely. Hardship will invade our world and miracles may or may not come, but in every circumstance Jesus will always be Christ. That truth is enough to create faith that can withstand anything.

It's inevitable that you, like John the Baptist, will one day have some crisis of faith. There will come a time—maybe even today—when you must face a great question, one with eternal consequences, one to which you just don't know the answer. When that moment comes, don't look desperately for a miracle. Don't demand some temporary hope or ill-thought solution. Instead, cling inseparably to Christ, the substance of your hope. Whisper your worries into his ear. Show him the tattered remains of your faith. Weep just a bit on his strong shoulders, if you need to. Ask him the hard questions. And then surrender yourself completely to his power and to his presence in your life.

Amen!

SEVEN

BEAUTIFUL SORROW

Why'd you have to wait? Where were you? Where were you?

—THE FRAY[1]

And God shall wipe away all tears from their eyes.

—REVELATION 21:4 KJV

n Bethany, about two miles east of Jerusalem, there lived a small family made up of Lazarus—the head of the house—and his two sisters, Mary and Martha. What made these three unique was that they were close friends of Jesus. Powerful company to keep! And then . . .

While Jesus was about a day's journey away from Bethany, Lazarus became very ill—sick to the point of death. Mary and Martha hurriedly dispatched a messenger to Friend Jesus: "Lord, the one you love is sick," they told him (John 11:3). Surely he who healed the blind and deaf and lame and more, surely he who loved his confidant and friend, surely he for whom compassion was commonplace—that Lord Jesus would come quickly to the aid of Lazarus, right?

Well, wrong.

Jesus refused to come, all the while knowing that any delay was deadly. And while Christ was away, Lazarus died. Days later, with Lazarus long gone and buried, Christ finally pulled up his entourage in Bethany. Too late. Much too late.

Now, if you've read your Bible or even attended Sunday school as a child, you know what comes next is an awe-inspiring, miraculous happy ending. Jesus stands in front of Lazarus's tomb, commands the dead man back to life, and rights all wrongs. Joy to all!

Except . . . when I witness this vision of God's power and compassion I can't help getting hung up on what happened *before* the miracle.

For four long days before Christ arrived—four choking, hopeless days spent waiting while Jesus dawdled nearby—Mary, Martha, and anyone who loved Lazarus was plunged into deep despair. Look, Jesus wasn't just late; he was deliberately tardy. Jesus didn't just let death happen; he made sure it happened.

Our sisters had dutifully trusted in Christ, hoped in him, placed their brother's life in his hands, literally begged for his presence in the midst of their tragedy.

But Jesus didn't come.

How's that for disappointment with God?

The Open Secret: You Are Destined for Sorrow

I read recently about a political polling firm that asked people to give an "approval rating" for God. Apparently the Big Guy's got reason for concern, because a little more than half—52 percent—of American voters approve of his "overall dealings" with people.[2] Were Mary and Martha a part of that poll's results, my guess is that they'd have fallen in with the roughly 48 percent who have marked reservations about how God handles things in this fine universe of his.

I'd be willing to bet that you, too, at times have not approved of God's dealings in your life. I know that's been true of me. How could it not be that way? This world hurts, and when sorrow grips the day, regardless of the truth of any situation, it often feels as though God is deliberately late, that he's simply decided not to care, not to help, not even to make his presence known.

Why does Christ allow—and perhaps insist?—that his followers, his *friends*, endure suffering. Were I a more capable thinker, maybe I could give you a solid, theological, comforting answer to that question.[3] But I'm going to be honest with you: I don't know why we're required to live through sorrows in this life, and I'm not going to pretend that I do. My editor tells me I should at least offer up a thought or two on this, so maybe it's an issue of growth, a way to prepare us for eternity. Maybe it's simply a long-lasting, awful consequence of sin. Maybe it's that you and I just deserve worse and fail to see God's mercy in our pain.

Whatever the reason, let's just admit the obvious, shall we?

Just like Mary and Martha and even Lazarus, you and I are destined for sorrow.

There is no exemption for heartbreak in the human race. Grief defines us; it hovers over and behind every moment of life. No, of course we aren't constantly grieving the death of a loved one, but we grieve more than simply loss of life. We grieve loss of hope, loss of opportunity, loss of security, loss of innocence, loss of relationship, and much more. Sometimes we grieve when we just wake up and feel—for no good reason—that something has gone from life that we loved but can never recapture.

One of my favorite movies is Steve Carell's underappreciated gem *Dan in Real Life*. What I like best from the whole film is the first fifteen seconds of Carell's performance as the title character.

The movie opens on Dan sleeping. He wakes up alone and in silence, surrounded by the detritus of unfinished, overwhelming obligations from yesterday. In the empty bedroom, Dan shrugs off the bedcovers and sits up, feet on the floor. And there he pauses. Head down. Shoulders bowed. Hands gripping his knees.

A deep breath. A sigh of resignation. A summoning once more of just enough courage to face another day.

"Okay," he says finally.

Then he stands, walks off scene and into the rest of the film. Many things happen from that point on, but whenever I see him after that, I always see in his eyes *that* Dan—the guy who needs everything within him just to get out of bed in the morning.[4]

Been there. Done that.

How 'bout you?

C. S. Lewis apparently knew that feeling well. In 1959, as his wife, ironically named Joy, was suffering from the debilitating cancer that would eventually kill her, he wrote to a friend asking for redoubled prayer. "The dreadful thing, as you know," he confessed helplessly, "is the waking each morning—the moment at which it all flows back on one."[5]

I suspect that, when Lazarus's illness worsened and then turned to death, Mary and Martha knew intimately what Dan and C. S. Lewis and you and I have all experienced: the cold, pale light of morning filled with loss of hope and theft of joy. In reality, Mary and Martha likely entered that phase barely hours after sending to Jesus for help.

On day one, the timetable seems to indicate, the messenger is sent and Lazarus dies. Day two, Jesus dawdles, deliberately putting off action, despite the urgency of the call. Day three, Jesus finally starts walking toward Bethany. Day four, he arrives late in the day and is informed of what he already knew: Lazarus is dead, and has been for four full days.[6]

And for each of those four days, Mary and Martha were forced to live with the crushing disappointment of being overlooked by God, to awake from restless, exhausted sleep and experience once more that "moment at which it all flows back on one."

My brother is dead.

My Savior didn't come.

I am alone and bereft in this world.

It Is No Sin to Feel Sad

When C. S. Lewis's wife, Joy, finally passed away in 1960, it was not just the beginning of Lewis's grief but the peak of it. Lewis's stepson, Douglas Gresham, explains in the introduction to *A Grief Observed*, "When Jack [C. S. Lewis's nickname] was racked with the emotional pain of his bereavement, he also suffered the mental anguish resulting from three years of living in constant fear . . . and the sheer exhaustion of spending those last few weeks in constant caring for his dying wife."[7]

In the days and weeks following Joy's death, Jack took to writing down his pain as a means of survival, never intending that anyone other than himself would read it. The result was four short manuscript books filled with Lewis's agony and redemption. Those handwritten notes were beautifully raw and difficult and honest, something that Gresham called "a man emotionally naked in his own Gethsemane."[8]

"No one ever told me that grief felt so like fear," Lewis began his first journal.

I am not afraid, but the sensation is like being afraid. The same fluttering in the stomach, the same restlessness, the yawning. I keep on swallowing. . . .

Meanwhile, where is God? This is one of the most disquieting symptoms. When you are happy, so happy that you have no sense of needing Him, so happy that you are tempted to feel His claims upon you as an interruption, if you remember yourself and turn to Him with gratitude and praise, you will be—or so it feels—welcomed with open arms. But go to Him when your need is desperate, when all other help is vain, and what do you find? A door slammed in your face, and a sound of bolting and double bolting on the inside. After that, silence. You may as well turn away. The longer you wait, the more emphatic the silence will become. . . . Why is He so present a commander in our time of prosperity and so very absent in times of trouble?[9]

I have known those who would frown at C. S. Lewis and his honesty here.

"God works all things for good," they'd say—and they are right (Romans 8:28). But knowing that doesn't make pain easier to endure, not at first anyway.

I've known those who would chide Lewis and tell him to buck up, who would point out that people have died throughout human history, that he had known for years that his wife's illness would kill her, and that Joy's death was all part of God's eternal plan. They would judge him as immature, as ungrateful for choosing to focus on his sorrow instead of the blessing Joy had been in his life.

I don't know about you, but I often feel like smacking those kinds of people.

I've known folks who would be mildly embarrassed by the naked display of sorrow in Jack's intimate journal, who would suggest that he hurry his way through grief so he could get back to "normal" and move on with his life. I'm embarrassed to say that, on occasion, I've been that kind of person.

Thank God that Jack Lewis knew something that Lazarus's sisters also figured out a few millennia ago: it is no sin to feel sadness.

It's not wrong to express honest disappointment with your Savior. It is not wrong to be naked and helpless in his sight. It's not wrong to tell him what he already knows about the way you feel.

When Tardy Jesus finally showed up in Bethany, the response of Lazarus's sisters is, well, both heartbreaking and beautiful.

At home, in the company of friends sharing their grief, Mary and Martha hear that Jesus is just outside, a little ways up the road, heading to their home. Martha immediately rushes out to meet him. Mary stays behind. Why? Maybe she's angry. Maybe she's hurt by Christ's delay. Maybe she simply can't face him right now . . . and thinking maybe that serves him right. I've felt that way toward God at times, tried to give him a silent treatment of sorts. It didn't do me much good, but I can't deny I felt it.

Meanwhile, Martha meets Jesus in the road, and her first words to him are words of sorrow and accusation of complicity. "Lord," she says, "if you had been here, my brother would not have died" (John 11:21).

It's interesting that Jesus never rebukes her for this sorrow, or for her accusation that he had failed. Instead, he reaches into her grief with a promise, "Your brother will rise again," and then gently points her back to faith. "I am the resurrection and the life. The one who believes in me will live, even though they die" (John 11:23, 25). Basically, "In spite of your brother's death, do you still trust me?"

Why didn't Jesus rebuke her for lack of faith? Tell her to stop blubbering and to start living? Why didn't he frown and tell her to get hold of herself? I'd guess it's because God's not intimidated or threatened by honest emotion; because it was no sin for Martha to feel sad at the loss of her brother—even when that sadness was multiplied by a perception that God had let her down.

I have a friend, let's call him Clark, who sometimes struggles with bouts of depression. He wrote to me once to ask my advice about that. Clark was on an emotional loop that went something like this: "I feel sad, sometimes for a reason, sometimes for no reason at all. And then I worry because I can't make myself stop feeling sad, and I can't tell anyone about it because depression isn't something polite people talk about. And then I get even more depressed because I can't stop being depressed . . . and so I feel sad."

I'm no psychologist. I don't know the ins and outs of medical treatment for depression. But I do know this: sometimes I feel sad too, and no amount of telling myself not to feel sad helps me not feel sad. So you know what I do? I tell Jesus, *Lord, I'm depressed. Do something about it.* And then I get on with my life.

Do I stop being depressed right away? Nope, not usually. But I refuse to let depression be the thing that stops me from trusting God's faithfulness, or from loving my wife, or from putting in a good day's work, or from hanging out and playing games with my son and his family, or from going to the movies with my nieces, or whatever. So that's what I told my friend. Go ahead and feel sad, but don't let that sadness keep you from living, or from finding joy in the little happinesses of life.

When I got Clark's return e-mail, I could almost hear the relief in his words, "I feel so much better," he said to me, "just knowing that it's okay to feel bad sometimes!"

So let me tell you now, just in case you didn't know it: it's okay to feel bad sometimes, to be depressed, to feel overwhelmed and like giving up.

It's okay to turn to Jesus and say, "Lord, if you had been here, my husband would never have left me . . . I wouldn't have this chronic illness . . . the terrorist attack would have been prevented," and so on.

As I see it, the only real problems with sorrow are when you allow it to prevent you from *living*, or when you use it as punishment either for yourself or for someone else. For instance, grief as penance for guilt is unhealthy, but you need to deal with your guilt before you can deal with your grief. Grief as an excuse to opt out of relationships or as a means of controlling them is a problem. You don't need to punish yourself with sorrow, but you must allow yourself to experience sorrow—simply because it's going to be present in some way in just about every day of your life.

Listen to how Lewis described that: "As to how I take sorrow, the answer is 'in nearly all the possible ways.' Because, as you probably know, it isn't a state, but a process. It keeps on changing—like a winding road with quite a new landscape at each bend."[10]

And that leads me to something we must learn to admit about our Lord:

Jesus Is a Man of Sorrows

Isaiah gave this prophetic description of Jesus Christ: "He was despised and rejected by men; a man of sorrows, and acquainted with grief" (Isaiah 53:3 ESV).

Perhaps that's why Jesus didn't rebuke Martha when she poured out her grief on him. And when Mary later came to him weeping, accusing, he didn't reprimand her either. Do you know what he did instead?

He cried with her (John 11:32–35).

I've always had trouble with that. Why did Jesus cry? He wasn't surprised by the loss of Lazarus. He knew Lazarus was dead before he ever set out to visit Bethany, and he planned ahead to work that miracle of resurrection. "Our friend Lazarus has fallen asleep," he told his disciples plainly, "but I am going there to wake him up" (John 11:11).

So why the tears?

The creator of life was clearly not overwhelmed by the death of Lazarus. He knew the endgame. He fully intended, in just moments, to change all tears to laughter. With one simple command, he was going to bring Lazarus stumbling back from the grave. Yet he cried anyway. Why? Scripture gives a few clues. First, "He was . . . a man of sorrows, and acquainted with grief" (Isaiah 53:3 ESV).

Christ alone has experienced the fullness of grief both as limitless deity and as limited man. Thus Christ alone has perfect empathy for those of us who also find ourselves wrapped up in sorrow. Why did Jesus cry? Maybe it was just because Mary was crying. Because he understood perfectly what the apostle Paul would later mean when he said, "Rejoice with those who rejoice; weep with those who weep" (Romans 12:15 HCSB).

Second, "Jesus wept. Then the Jews said, 'See how he loved him!'" (John 11:35–36).

In *A Grief Observed*, Lewis suggests that bereavement is an inherent part of the experience of love, as natural as summer giving way to autumn.[11] If this is true, then only love truly has the power to grieve, because only love can care enough to feel the loss of an object of love. In that respect, it can honestly be said that in some intangible way and to some intangible degree, sorrow is evidence of love—or at least of the capacity to love.

For instance, I will tell you now that four years ago my aged dog died. Does that last sentence cause you feelings of sorrow? Does it make your throat feel tight, cause you to take a deep breath, make your eyes redden, and threaten a new headache from holding back tears? Of course not. You neither knew nor loved my little dog. But just thinking of that animal's passing—more than four years ago!—still causes very real pangs of sorrow in my heart. Why? Because I loved that dog, and my love still grieves his loss.

"See how he loved him!" they said when Jesus wept. And that, it seems, is a clue for us.

Jesus wept because he loved.

Knowing that a miracle was to come didn't prevent Christ from experiencing love and its correlating grief on behalf of Mary and Martha. Jesus' empathetic sorrow reveals his great capacity for love in the in-between moments, in the underneath places where sadness fills the cracks. Yes, very soon he will work a miracle, but until then, he is still a man of sorrows, filled with great love for those who mourn.

And so, because he loves, he weeps.

I admire what Mary did here. No, not the petulant part where she hid herself from Jesus out of anger or grief or whatever. I love that at last she did what you and I would always do if we were anything but selfish, shortsighted creatures.

She literally laid her sorrow at Jesus' feet.

"When Mary reached the place where Jesus was and saw him," John reports, "she fell at his feet and said, 'Lord, if you had been here, my brother would not have died'" (John 11:32).

Earlier I told you a hard truth, didn't I? You are destined for sorrow. Well, let me admit now that I told you only part of that truth. Here it is in full: you are destined for sorrow, but you never have to face any sadness alone.

In the heart of every sorrow, in the hidden moments of greatest grief, Jesus is always ready and willing to weep with you. And it is our unfathomable privilege to lay every ounce of sadness directly at his feet. He will always receive it, and like a faithful friend, he will always help to bear the unyielding burden it lays upon us, no matter how long it must be borne, or how often we return to his feet with our pain. Perhaps that's why the apostle Paul could say with such confidence, "We are pressured in every way but not crushed; we are perplexed but not in despair; we are persecuted but not abandoned; we are struck down but not destroyed" (2 Corinthians 4:8–9 HCSB).

Remember my friend Clark whom I told you about earlier? The one who sometimes struggles with depression? He has been an expression of this Friend Jesus in my life more than once, especially when I was living underneath the shade of sorrow. I remember one time specifically when I was a young man. I went to Clark because, as usual, a beautiful girl had broken my heart. He listened while I wailed, until I finally shuttered myself into silent tears. Then he did the craziest, most wonderful thing.

Without saying a word, Clark stood up and wrapped me in a hug. We stood there, me crying, him hugging, neither speaking. And then he let go and we both just sat in silence for a while. And somewhere in the silence of Clark's presence, I heard the whisper of Jesus reminding me that I was not alone—and I never would be, no matter what sorrows would come into my life.

At the exact moment I needed it, Christ, in his great love, had made sure I had a friend who would be more loyal to me than a faithful wind. And as the days and weeks and years have gone by, I've found the Man of Sorrows whispering comfort to me again and again in the silences of suffering. And slowly, slowly, I am learning to follow Mary's example, to drop myself at Jesus' feet and pour out my tears upon him.

"When Jesus saw her weeping, and the Jews who had come along with her also weeping, he was deeply moved" (John 11:33)

Why did Jesus cry? Because he loved Mary. Because the Man of Sorrows knew her grief. Because he refused to let her grieve alone, even for the precious few moments it would take until he worked a miracle that would turn her weeping into shouts of joy.

It's a beautiful picture, isn't it, to think that God has no need of weeping for you, but still loves enough to weep with you anyway?

And that hints at a mystery we sometimes miss when we're buried under the weight of depression and discouragement:

Sorrow Adds Texture to Beauty

Shortly after their marriage, Charles and Kate Dickens found themselves the guardians for Kate's younger sister, Mary Hogarth. Charles grew to love his young sister-in-law as if she were his own daughter, forging a deep familial friendship with her. He later declared that she was "the dear girl whom I loved, after my wife, more deeply and fervently than anyone on earth."

On Saturday night, May 6, 1837, the family happily attended the production of one of Charles's plays at the St. James Theatre. They came home in good spirits and then seventeen-year-old Mary fell suddenly, unexpectedly ill. Kate and Charles rushed to her side. The next day she was dead—she literally died in Charles's arms, "in such a calm and gentle sleep," Dickens later mourned, "that although I had held her in my arms for some time before, when she was certainly living (for she swallowed a little brandy from my hand) I continued to support her lifeless form, long after her soul had fled to Heaven."

The death of his sister-in-law transformed Charles Dickens—and his writing. For the rest of his life, he wore her ring on his own finger as a memory of her. And biographer Edgar Johnson reports,

> Out of his imagination [Mary] never died. Throughout almost his entire literary career his novels continue to reveal glimpses of now one and now another aspect of her shining image. Mary's gaiety and tenderness animate loving, laughing Ruth Pinch in *Martin Chuzzlewit*. His vision of her nobler qualities recurs again and again, in Florence Dombey's devotion to her brother and father, in David Copperfield's serene and perhaps too perfect Agnes, in the sacrificial spirit of Little Dorrit. . . . It is impossible to exaggerate the significance of this early love and early sorrow for Dickens.[12]

It is tragic that Mary Hogarth died a young woman, that Charles Dickens mourned that loss for the rest of his life. And yet, that deep sorrow also became inerasable texture behind Dickens's enduring works of art, lending beauty and depth to nearly every effort. This is not to say that Mary's death was an acceptable price to pay for the literary result! But it is to say that there was beauty to be found in the sorrow that death created. Dickens found it, and we are all just a little bit better for it.

Mark Twain also was no stranger to sorrow. In 1858, "Mark Twain" was still just Samuel Clemens, a young steamship pilot working on the Mississippi River in a boat called the *Pennsylvania*. Thanks to Samuel's influence, the steamship hired his younger brother, Henry, to work as a "mud clerk" (errand boy) on the boat.

During Henry's sixth round-trip between St. Louis and New Orleans, an altercation broke out. Samuel, defending his brother, smacked their boss over the head with a heavy stool and threw in a few extra punches for good measure. When the boat docked in New Orleans, Samuel was kicked off the *Pennsylvania* and barred from ever returning. So Samuel and Henry made plans to take separate ships back to St. Louis, where they would reunite and find new work. Henry would finish out his duties on the *Pennsylvania*, and Samuel would follow two days later on a different boat.

Midway home, about sixty miles south of Memphis, an accidental explosion ripped through the *Pennsylvania*, fatally wounding Henry Clemens. He was taken to Memphis where, shortly after, Samuel stood vigil by his brother's side. On June 18, Samuel wrote a friend these words, "Long before this reaches you, my poor Henry,—my darling, my pride, my glory, my *all*, will have finished his blameless career and the light of my life will have gone out in utter darkness. Oh God! this is hard to bear."[13] On June 21, 1858, Henry Clemens was dead.

Biographer Jerome Loving writes,

The tragedy, only the first in a series of calamities to rain down upon this otherwise singularly successful American life, had a long-lasting impact on Sam Clemens and Mark Twain. Not only did Twain wait to use his river background in his fiction, but Clemens never returned to the river as a pilot after 1861. He often said that he wanted to return and that piloting for him would have been the most satisfying career in the world, but he no more wanted to return to the river.[14]

Out of Samuel Clemens's unspeakable grief came more than just a career change from steamship pilot to literary icon. That heartbreaking experience colored the rest of his life—and his work. Twain's stories of life on the Mississippi River are all populated and textured by the author's memories of sailing that river with his brother, Henry. And in those stories we've gained breathtaking glimpses of Americana, of muddled heroes and heroic humanity, of timeless joy and beautiful sorrow. Like Dickens, Mark Twain found beauty in his suffering, and generations have shared in the benefit.

Sorrow Is Prelude to Joy

Jesus wept.

Do you see the tears in his eyes? Do you feel the compassion of his words, the comfort of his presence?

Yes, it's tragic that Lazarus died, that Mary and Martha were left to grieve for four full days before Christ came with a miracle of life. And yet, the deep sorrow of those two sisters has also become more than simple sadness. Those tears have become texture behind the beauty of our Christ and of our understanding of God throughout history ever since.

Jesus wept. And that's just beautiful. Then, in the midst of the weeping, in the firm grasp of sorrow, Jesus did the unthinkable: he brought forth joy.

Standing in front of the tomb, he called out in a loud voice, "Lazarus, come out!" And do you know what happened? "The dead man came out" (John 11:43–44).

Can you imagine the unfiltered joy that followed Lazarus's postmortem appearance?

Can you see Martha's jaw drop, Mary's face transform with wide-eyed wonder?

Can you hear the cheers and shouts, the sobs of happiness?

Can you feel the trembling strength in the hugs the sisters place on their dearly departed, dearly returned brother?

Incomprehensible, indefensible joy.

And a reminder that, miracle or no, all of today's sorrows are at worst a shadowy prelude to tomorrow's joy. Even in our darkest moments we can experience mirrored reflections of that joy here and now. Ah, but when eternity finally comes? We will embrace it in *full*.

Somebody say *amen*!

Now, unlike Mary and Martha, I've not been present for the rapturous delight of a resurrection—but I have sampled a small taste of that kind of joy, of the laughter that somehow miraculously followed my tears. This hurtful, hateful world is not the end of me. There's better waiting on the horizon. And here's my little secret: I've an inkling of what's coming.

It happened when I was a freshman in college, visiting my grandfather on a quick trip home. We sat in his living room, and my grandfather was laughing so hard that tears streamed down his face like little rivers of joy staining his cheeks.

It was hard to believe he had buried his mother just a few hours earlier.

But that was my grandfather, a man we called "Jidee," and a man who chose to mix a little joy into the drink we called grief.

They'd been close, Jidee and my great-grandmother. He'd cared for her for many years, faithfully stopping by her home each day to see that she was warm and fed. He planned each day around seeing his mother. She lived a long, full life.

When the day came for her to leave this earth, my grandfather called me at college. "Please come home for the funeral," he said. "I'll pay for your plane ticket." I came, and my sisters and I all cried tears of sorrow during the service.

Later, exhausted, we retreated to Jidee's house. As we sat in somber silence, a smile flickered on my grandfather's face. He was remembering those special times a mother shares with her son. Curious, we begged him to tell us about growing up as an immigrant in the early 1900s.

For the next two hours he regaled us with stories of his mother, his brother, his aunts and uncles. We laughed and cried and shouted and sighed and mourned and rejoiced all at the same time. And it was a beautiful kind of sorrow, an image I've never forgotten and never gotten over.

A few decades later I sat in that same living room preparing for my beloved Jidee's funeral. In my head, I began telling my own stories about growing up with my grandfather, and through them all, through the funeral and long afterward, I kept seeing his face—the one I'd seen at my great-grandmother's funeral.

Laughing and crying. Mourning death and rejoicing life at the same time.

That's the picture of my grandfather that stays with me today, that moment when he taught me irreparably that there is joy to be found even in the midst of sorrow.

Take heart. The words of the psalmist are true. My grandfather smiled it. Mary and Martha testified to it. Jesus incredibly lived it. And I've even seen it with my own eyes.

> *Weeping may endure for a night,*
> *But joy cometh in the morning!*
>
> (Psalm 30:5 KJV, emphasis added)

EIGHT

INSULTING GREATNESS

*In this world, with great power there must
also come—great responsibility.*

—STAN LEE, MARVEL COMICS[1]

The Son of Man did not come to be served, but to serve.

—MARK 10:45

Nowadays, if you're looking for a good way to insult somebody, just order coffee.

Of course this won't work with the barista at your local Starbucks or your waitress at dinner tonight, but for pretty much everybody else it's a nice go-to move when you feel like being viewed as a big jerk.

Try it tomorrow at work and you'll see what I'm talking about.

Instead of saying "Good morning!" when you first see your boss, walk up to her and say, "I'll have a medium café au lait, with a little cinnamon dusted on top." Then, for extra fun, turn slightly away and make a shooing motion with your hands while you say, "And be quick about it—daylight's a-burnin'."

If your boss is the polite type, she'll probably take a moment to explain to you—quite effectively—that getting coffee is *not* in her job description, but it can easily be added to yours. If your boss is the other type, well, chances are good you'll get an impassioned instruction to "Get your own *bleeping* coffee!"

Hey, but maybe your boss is just cranky, right? So go ahead and try it on the street. Walk up to that construction worker over there and order a large decaf with soy milk and just a dab of foam. If you manage to avoid getting brained by a blunt instrument, turn your attention next to the pedestrian headed toward the bus stop. Perhaps, if you insist, that guy will get you a Manhattan-style cuppa joe—with cream and sugar. No? He gave you a rude gesture instead? Success! You've now become an insulting jerk!

You see the absurdity of this exercise, I'm sure. But do you see *why* demanding a cup of coffee can be so insulting? The problem is not one of content or ability—it's one of station. The reason is this: any act of service is inherently demeaning.

Regardless of how large or small an act of service is, it requires that the serving person—for that moment at least—subordinate himself or herself to the one being served.

Similarly, in first-century Israel, there were many comparable ways of insulting someone. But if you *really* wanted to offend—if you really wanted to shockingly heap scorn on an enemy, to demean him as utterly inferior to you, all you had to do was this:

Order him to wash your feet.

The Greatest Insult

Foot washing in the ancient world was such a degrading act that the modern insult of ordering coffee is really only a pale comparison. A more culturally sympatric insult would be, say, if I suggested that your station in life was to clean prison toilets six days a week, twelve hours a day.

In the ancient world, no free man would ever have been expected to do something as demeaning as wash another's feet. Foot washing was necessary, yes, but most people handled that chore themselves, much the same way we today take care of our own bathroom business.[2] In more affluent families, though, the dirty duty of foot washing could be dumped on a slave. In that case, the luckless servant would stand by the door with a basin of water and a towel, consigned to the indignity of scrubbing the filthy feet of traveling guests who entered the home. Even then, in an honorable Hebrew household, only a Gentile slave would be stationed by the door with that chore—Jewish slaves were considered too good for that degrading act![3]

What's more, just mimicking the appearance of this kind of menial slave was cause for shame. For instance, when Roman emperor Caligula wanted to humiliate a few of his political enemies in the senate, he famously forced them to ape the attire of foot-washing slaves and to wait on him as mock servants.[4] The insult was obvious and profound. It's no surprise, then, that Caligula's senate enemies plotted to shorten that ruler's reign! Using one of Caligula's own bodyguards as the hit man, they had their emperor murdered in AD 41—less than four years after he ascended to power.[5]

It's this kind of cultural context that makes Jesus' actions on the night before his execution so hard to grasp, even today, thousands of years after they occurred. The Bible records the scandalous story in John 13:1–17. You know the short version: Jesus washed his disciples' feet. But do you comprehend the revulsion of that single sentence? Do you appreciate the living insult that Jesus embodied in that moment? Are you really aware of how grossly inappropriate his actions were in that place and time? According to theologian Lawrence Richards, "Christ's act . . . within the context of first-century Judaism, was truly shocking—an absolutely stunning example."[6]

It happened during the meal we now call the Last Supper, just hours before Christ's arrest and execution. Picture it with me.

It was evening, nearing the end of a long, crazy week.

On Sunday, they'd arrived in Jerusalem to a hero's welcome. No, more than a hero—it was a welcome fit for a king. Peter, John, and the other disciples watched in joyful amazement as the crowds pressed in to greet them. So many people—so many! And all of them cheering, shouting, rocking the entire city with their noise. All of them bellowing out praise for Jesus of Nazareth.

"Hosanna! Save us!"

"Blessed!"

"Hosanna in the highest!"

People ran joyously ahead of them in the streets, spreading coats and cloaks and freshly cut tree boughs, creating a carpet of glory for their Messiah. The disciples followed Jesus down that carpet, through that cheering crowd, and they felt the warmth of truth.

Jesus *belonged* here.

This was no overhyped procession. This was God in the flesh, coming to bring salvation to all who would believe.

It was Sunday, and for today at least, it felt good.

Monday was even more crazy, if that was possible. Jesus, the coming king, walked into the temple and did what no other religious leader had the guts to do: throw the crooked scoundrels out. He went nuts! He kicked over the tables of corrupt money-grubbers who'd set up shop there. He whipped the temple into a frenzy, shouting judgment on those who would turn his house of prayer into a "den of robbers" (Matthew 21:13).

It was glorious.

And then, when the temple had been cleansed, he unclenched

his fists and opened his hands, reaching gently to touch the blind and the lame, and healing them. One miracle after another, the literal power of God flowing freely in the lives of everyday people. Not even the children could contain themselves anymore. "Hosanna!" they shouted as they danced through the temple courtyard, "Hosanna to the Son of David" (Matthew 21:15).

Tuesday and Wednesday were a whirlwind of activity. The crowds kept coming. Jesus taught them of God. He healed the sick. He rebuked the self-righteous hypocrites and let real truth rain down on them in judgment. This was truly the Son of God, the hoped-for Messiah, the King of kings! His every word and every action was unmistakable evidence of that.[7]

And now, on Thursday, exhausted, the disciples and Jesus had gathered in the Upper Room to celebrate the Passover feast. Sundown marked the transition from Thursday to Friday, and then the Passover began. The group finally had a moment to breathe, to revel in the experiences of the past few days, to sit in awe at the nearness of one such as Jesus Christ.

The King.

The Messiah.

The Son of . . . wait a minute.

What is he . . . was that a towel?

Oh no . . . not that.

What is Jesus doing?

And there he was, Jesus the Christ, God incarnate, doing the unthinkable.

He got up from the meal. He took off his outer clothing. He wrapped a towel around his waist, girding himself like the lowest of Gentile slaves, keeping one long end of the towel free for menial use. Then he poured water into a basin and began to—was he really doing this?—wash his disciples' feet, drying them with the towel that was wrapped around him (John 13:4–5). How degrading. How humiliating. How terribly uncomfortable for everyone reclining at the table.

No one spoke at first. No one dared. What do you say when your Lord and Master, your teacher and hero, becomes a living insult? When he ignores everything that's happened previously in this week and suddenly acts like *that*?

This, it seemed, was going to change everything.

Greatness Is the DNA of Service

Jesus washed his disciples' feet.

Can you see the unbelievable incongruity—and raw power—of that image? Do you see the casual greatness and inexpressible love this reveals?

I feel uncomfortable writing about this scene from Jesus' life on earth because in it I see all that I will never become, at least not in this lifetime.

There sits the unequaled, eternal Son of God, stationing himself underneath despoiled and transitory things, sullied by the dirty feet of others, yet unstained by anything that dares to rise above him. Meanwhile here I sit, arrogantly appalled that God would debase himself like a lowly slave—and scared because I know he asks me to essentially do the same.

I'm of Middle Eastern descent. My great-grandfather came to America about a hundred years ago, and we've been here ever since. While that has many cultural advantages, one of the disadvantages is that well-meaning Christian people frequently ask me to play Jesus in church pageants and Easter parades and Sunday school videos and so on. I always say no to those requests, and I always will. John 13:1–17 is the perfect example why: I can never even pretend to be the kind of person who would willingly step down from eternity and into the sandals of a foot-washing slave. That kind of greatness not only eludes me, it's incomprehensible to me. I wouldn't have the slightest clue how to portray a person like that, even in fiction. It's hard enough for me to deal with it in real life.

Jesus washed his disciples' feet.

There have been great men and women throughout history. There have been great deeds as well. But only one was able to take the ultimate insult of his time and turn it into an image of greatness that lasts forever. Only Jesus could do that—embody greatness of service—because only Jesus is truly great. And that leads me to mention something important that this moment reveals for us: greatness is the essence of service.

I've often heard it preached that you and I become great by serving others, and I suppose there's probably an element of truth to that. But the example of Jesus tells me that maybe we've made a mistake in our understanding of the true nature of greatness and the inseparable idea of service. Listen to what John wrote about this: "Jesus knew that the Father had put all things under his power, and that he had come from God and was returning to God; so he got up from the meal, took off his outer clothing, and wrapped a towel around his waist" (John 13:3–4).

Jesus knew who he was, knew there was nothing and no one in all creation who was his equal . . . *so* . . . he got up from the meal and started washing his disciples' feet. As one theologian explains it, "Jesus did what he did because he knew what he knew."[8]

Do you see what that means? Jesus didn't serve in order to show he was great; he served *because* he is great—and because he knew it all along. His greatness was the catalyst for his service. "Jesus knew . . . *so* he got up." Christ's humiliating act of service was, in a miraculous, mystifying way, normal. It's simply part of Almighty God's person. Jesus demonstrated that greatness is the natural source of the attitude of service, not vice versa.

Luke 9:48 lends additional credence to this perspective. "It is the one who is least among you all," Jesus taught his followers, "who is the greatest." Notice Christ didn't say, "the least among you *will become* the greatest" or "the least of you will *earn* greatness." The tense used here is present, describing a state that currently exists, that existed prior to, and also continuously through, any action of service.

"The one who *is* least . . . *is* the greatest."

Perhaps that's why Jesus could say so easily about himself, "The Son of Man did not come to be served, but to serve" (Mark 10:45). And why he could so easily don the towel and carry the basin to wash his followers' filthy feet.

One is not great because he serves; one serves because he is great.

So what does this mean? Yes, we're to pursue service in our lives, that's obvious. But if we're serving because we hope to impress God, to become great in his sight, to earn his favor, well, we're really just wasting our time. If we think this way, we must not know—or believe—that through Christ, you and I are already great in God's sight. Listen:

You are God's very own child (John 1:12–13). You are his new creation (2 Corinthians 5:17). You are inseparable from his love (Romans 8:35–39). You are a citizen of heaven (Philippians

3:20). You are God's living temple (1 Corinthians 3:16). You are God's creative craftsmanship (Ephesians 2:10). You can do all things through Christ (Philippians 4:13). How could anyone who is all those things and more be anything less than great?

You and I, we're not great because we serve. Like Jesus, we serve because we're great, because greatness lives within us, and because serving is the nature of greatness. Coursing through our veins, flooding our minds, and permeating our very souls is the unmatchable greatness of God in us. The question, then, is not whether we might gain some random glory from serving, or earn some higher heavenly rank through service. The question is, how much of our current, God-given greatness are we going to release freely into our world?

Greatness Reaches Across Enemy Lines to Serve

Of course, serving out of your greatness is not easy.

Truth is, in this sin-stained world of ours, it's often hard and sometimes heartbreaking. But greatness is not limited to friendly territory or safe opportunities. Greatness serves because of who the server is, not because of who is being served. Nowhere is this more obvious than around the table at the Last Supper.

"He poured water into a basin and began to wash his disciples' feet."

That included the pillars of our faith like Peter and John, who wrote down what happened.

And Judas Iscariot.

History's worst criminal—the man who betrayed Jesus and set in motion the events that led to Christ's arrest, to his torture, and crucifixion. Jesus' worst human enemy sat in the circle and let the Messiah wash his feet. Some early traditions in church history have even speculated that Judas's feet were the first ones Jesus washed.[9]

John 13:2 makes it clear that Judas was among Jesus' disciples at this Passover feast. And, just for emphasis I guess, John reminds us of Judas's presence again after the foot washing, in verse 10. What's more, John reveals in verse 11, "He [Jesus] knew who was going to betray him."

Christ knew Judas was his self-appointed enemy, and Jesus still washed Judas's feet.

Greatness serves because of who the server is, not because of who is being served. Sometimes greatness must reach across enemy lines in order to serve.

The great Renaissance artist Michelangelo experienced that kind of difficulty firsthand early in his career, when his worst enemy was the man who should have been his greatest friend. Piero di Lorenzo de' Medici was the eldest son of Duke Lorenzo de' Medici, and he'd taken over his father's title and household upon the old man's death—inheriting with it the role of benefactor to the promising young artist Michelangelo Buonarroti.

In that day an artist needed a patron—that is, a wealthy person who sponsored art projects and paid for living and material expenses for the artist. This allowed someone like Michelangelo to concentrate solely on his art instead of working at peasant labor to earn money for food. For many years, Michelangelo had been fortunate enough to have the powerful Duke Lorenzo as his patron. It was Lorenzo who had first discovered his talent as a sculptor and who invited Michelangelo to live in his palace as part of his household. It was Lorenzo who had become the young man's friend and provided block after block of the finest marble to use for his exquisite carvings.

But then Lorenzo was gone, and the brutish Piero ruled in his place. The son let Michelangelo continue to live on the palace grounds, but he disdained the artist's work, mocking him and leaving him to languish in empty solitude.

One wintry day in 1494, Michelangelo had been sitting by a window watching the snow fall silently on the ground outside when Duke Piero sent a servant to call for him. When he arrived in the duke's presence, it was painfully clear why the artist had been summoned: Piero had guests, and he wanted to impress them by humiliating the supposedly great sculptor living on his grounds.

"Today we have need of your talent," Piero announced in a mocking tone. "You do have great talent, do you not, my friend?"

Turning toward a large window and pointing to the snow-covered countryside, the Duke continued, "I am giving a dinner tonight, and I want my guests to be able to see one of your brilliant statues. You will go down to the garden. There you will find all the white marble your heart desires, lying heaped upon the ground. Of course, tomorrow morning the sun will do away with all your hard labor. But nothing lasts forever, does it, young maestro?"

Snickers broke out among the crowd of Piero's friends as the reality of the command set in. This new Duke of Medici wanted a sculpture made out of snow—knowing it would melt away to nothing by the next day! Red-hot anger and embarrassment flushed through Michelangelo's body. This enemy was deliberately insulting the artist, simply to make himself look better in the eyes of his friends.

Michelangelo thought of walking away, of setting out to find a nobler patron somewhere else. He thought of simply refusing the Duke's command and returning to his room on the palace grounds. But he didn't. In the end, he simply responded with a promise to serve, saying, "I will do your bidding, O great Medici." Then he turned and went immediately out to the snow-covered garden.

For some time, Michel stared into the wintry wasteland before him. And he thought. And he dreamed. And before long he saw it, saw that thing no one else could even imagine, much less create.

He set to work.

Laboring in silence through the hardship of cold and loneliness and day giving way to night, he first spent long hours simply packing snow, packing snow, and packing more snow. Finally, he had before him a large, ice-hard, marble-like block to work with.

He was ready, with frozen hands and chilled limbs, to carve.

Caught up in his work, he began to bring exquisite detail out of the block of ice. A head first. Then shoulders and a torso. Hands and feet. Back to the head where the face must be formed, where life must be animated with detailed precision.

And so he worked, and at some point in the frozen drudgery, a miracle happened. Out of the emptiness of snow and ice and frost and cruel patrons and undeserved enemies, beauty was formed. A sublime piece of art, forged as if by magic, out of icy snow.

Exhausted in the early evening, Michelangelo at last stood back to evaluate his work. Unexpectedly, he heard an astonished gasp.

Unknown to him, Duke Piero had stolen silently up beside

him and now stood gazing at the sculpted form in his snow-encrusted garden. His enemy's face was pained, hands palsied by more than just the cold.

"Snow," he whispered to his artist. "Not snow! Something this beautiful should never pass away . . ."

From that day forward, Michelangelo's greatest enemy became his greatest ally and patron. And the rest, as they say, is history.[10]

That angelic figure carved in snow for a noble's garden party has long been lost to the world, but the lesson of Michelangelo's snow-covered miracle has not. It speaks as a reflection of what Jesus revealed when he washed Judas Iscariot's dirty, disgusting feet—that sometimes greatness must be willing to reach across enemy lines in service. Yes, that can be insulting and unpleasant; but it also has the potential to create undeniable beauty in the lives of everyone involved.

Service Is Not Subservience

At this point, before you assume that I believe all Christians are obligated to live as doormats for all the awful people of the world—or even for the nice people of the world—it's important to point out one other principle about service that Jesus wonderfully embodied when he washed his disciples' feet. Service is not subservience.

Blind loyalty, unquestioning obedience to human authority, obsequious submissiveness—those things aren't true service. That type of "service" only seeks appeasement and approval and, perhaps, an avoidance of punishment. When service is defined this way, it leads inexorably to corruption and abuse—and it removes the servant's ability to freely act on behalf of the one served.

Biblical images of service, in both the Old and New Testaments, reject the idea that service demands subservience. Submission? Yes. Respect? Of course. But subservience? Incontrovertibly *no*. "Servants," Bible scholars tell us, "are called upon to have an attitude of deference to their superiors, to seek their benefit rather than to be self-seeking and to be obedient and useful."[11] In other words, true service seeks the best interests of the one served.

That simply doesn't happen if the servant is merely a posterior-kissing, subservient toad. The honest truth is that subservience is not only unhealthy for a servant, it's actually harmful for the one who is served. Why? Because it interferes with the servant's ability to fulfill the biblical vision of true service.

But wait! There's more.

The truly radical aspect that Jesus added to the definition of service was to insist, in both his example and teaching, that a Master was expected to serve the servants. Today thinkers in both business and religious circles call this concept "servant leadership," and we take for granted that everyone knows what that means. Before Jesus, however, that idea simply didn't exist—it was first born in the person of Christ. It is, literally, his invention.[12]

Leadership theorists label servant leadership as "ethical altruism." Dr. Peter Northouse of Western Michigan University explains what that means. "Leaders who serve are altruistic," he says. "They place their followers' welfare foremost in their plans. . . . Like health professionals, ethical leaders have a responsibility to attend to others, be of service to them, and make decisions pertaining to them that are beneficial and not harmful to their welfare."[13]

That kind of biblically centered, Christ-originated, radically powerful service doesn't look like subservience to me.

Yes, true service can be insulting—Jesus washing feet is testimony to that. Yes, true service can be degrading. It can be unpleasant. It's inherently demeaning in that it requires you to submit yourself to the authority of another. It often requires obedience without full understanding, and possibly without full agreement. Yes, all of that is true. But within that context you must understand this bedrock reality: true service is never—not ever—an act of subservience. Only self-aggrandizing bullies and self-righteous saps will tell you that it is.

In reality, sometimes the best service you can offer to another is to refuse to do the service that person demands of you. For instance, you are not serving an alcoholic by filling his cup with Jack Daniels because he commands it. Likewise, a doctor doesn't serve a patient by treating cancer with petunias just because the patient prefers flowers to chemotherapy.

Jesus washed his disciples' feet, and despite the obvious impropriety of that action, only one person at the table objected to it. As Christ worked his way through the group, he came eventually to Simon Peter, who, as could be expected, was appalled.

"No," Peter commanded Jesus, "you shall never wash my feet" (John 13:8).

Jesus, in the exact moment when he was deliberately showing himself as the perfect example of servanthood—when he was humbly subordinating himself to the men reclining around the Passover table—in that moment Christ refused to do what his authority figure asked him to do.

"You do not realize now what I am doing, but later you will understand," Jesus tried to explain. Peter didn't get it. So Christ got tough with Peter and his unreasonable command. "Unless I wash you," Jesus the Servant said, "you have no part with me."

"Then, Lord," Peter commanded his Christ-servant, "not just my feet but my hands and my head as well!" (John 13:7–9). It's hard to tell if Simon was being sarcastic or serious at that moment, but what isn't difficult to interpret was the Servant's reaction to the disciple's command.

In all, Christ the perfect servant refused three direct commands from Peter, the one whom he was at that moment determined to serve. Why? It's simple, really: Because service is not subservience. Because true service seeks the best interests of the one served. Because Jesus wasn't trying to win Peter's approval or accommodate his every whim. Because Jesus was seeking Peter's best interests and acting accordingly, whether Peter liked it or not.

If Christ had obeyed any of Peter's commands at that moment, then Jesus would've been acting against all his disciples' best interests, both short-term and long-term. And Christ was unwilling to do that. He knew better.

He loved better. He loved Peter enough to demand the best for him, even while serving him, even if that meant going against Peter's wishes.

Service Is Christ's Love in Fixed Form

In the world of copyright law, all ideas are public property. That's why there can be a thousand stories about a prince who rescues a princess, or boy wizards, or a couple that "meets cute," has a fight, and then lives happily ever after. Ownership of intellectual property—an idea—only begins when that idea is uniquely placed in what lawyers call "fixed form."

Let me explain.

Let's suppose that just this morning, while slurping down a bowl of Lucky Charms, I dreamed up a fantastic new story called "Brave Bryan Norman!" That'd be a pretty cool thing, right? However, just thinking up my story wouldn't grant me ownership of that abstract idea—not yet at least. In order for me to claim full copyright ownership of "Brave Bryan Norman!" I'd need to transfer that idea into *fixed form*—that is, into some "tangible medium of expression" that can be preserved in a way that's "perceptible either directly or with the aid of a machine or device."[14]

I'd need to embed "Brave Bryan Norman!" into a form that could be easily perceived by the human senses, for instance, writing it on paper, typing it into a computer file, speaking it into a digital recorder, painting it on a wall, or doing something that would fix my idea in humanly observable form. Only when my intangible idea is translated into something tangible and perceptible can people then rightly associate it with me as its creator.

Why do I tell you about that random legal concept? Now, stick with me on this . . . Because, to begin with, John 13:1 reveals that the prelude to Jesus' insulting act of washing the disciples' feet was this: "Having loved his own who were in the world, he [Jesus] now showed them the full extent of his love."

Having loved—Christ's great, intangible idea—he now showed in the tangible "fixed form" of service the full extent of his love. That's how service is Christ's love in fixed form.

In a single, menial act for his disciples, Jesus showed unequivocally and irrevocably that he loved them. He took his immeasurable, indescribable, intangible love and transferred it into a tangible medium of expression that his followers could perceive directly, with their senses. Through his service, Christ's love was made observable and perceptible to human touch and smell and sight and sound. He loved in fixed form, and finally, they got it, and we get it—Jesus *loves* us.

Yes, as I mentioned earlier, service is a natural outcome of greatness. That is remarkably true. But it's also more than just that. In service you and I are allowed to—invited to!—share tangibly in that exceedingly great, eternally abstract idea that God alone created and owns: Christ's everlasting love.

That helps me today, when I'm reading Jesus' concluding words in John 13:15. "I have set you an example," he said after washing the disciples' feet, "that you should do as I have done for you." I read those words and I feel truly discouraged, because I know myself and I know my sinful limitations. Can I actually live up to the insulting greatness of Jesus' act of service? Am I great enough to live a life of underneath kindness as Jesus did? I'm going to be honest with you. No.

I can't live up to that great call of service. Not really. Despite my lofty words and best efforts, I'm woefully inadequate.

But can I love?

Well . . .

Yeah. I think so.

I mean, everybody loves somebody, right? And if I can love another—friend or enemy or stranger or whomever—can I learn to express that love in fixed form, in some tangible act of service as Jesus did?

Um . . .

I think so? Well, yeah, with God's help, I can do that.

That's encouraging to me because it means that even though I'm no great servant in myself, Christ's love working in me is enough to help me be of great service. And because I suspect you often feel as inadequate as I do in this regard, I'll ask you the same question I ask myself each day. Can you love?

If so, then despite your varied shortcomings, you, too, can live out a Christlike life. A life full of service. A life of insulting greatness.

NINE

BRUTAL LOVE

Love . . . It's why super-heroes throw themselves headlong at impossible threats. Because their hearts overflow with it.

—AXEL ALONSO, MARVEL COMICS' EDITOR IN CHIEF[1]

It is finished.

—JOHN 19:30

f you happen to be traveling to Russia in the near future, and if you are observant type, you may be treated to a view of something really special.

You might find it on a bridge, hanging in a tree, or even attached to something as common as a gate or fence. My friends Thom and Joani Schultz found theirs unexpectedly while touring through the neverlands of the former USSR. It was situated by a lovely country road.

As they were passing this particularly scenic spot, Thom and Joani noticed a sparkling lake resting in the Russian countryside.

Surrounding the lake was a long metal fence.

And something on that fence caught Thom's eye. He had to take a closer look.

They stopped the car, got out, and began inspecting their surprising find. They peered closely at that random fence that circled a random lake, and what did they see?

Hundreds—maybe thousands—of padlocks.

All shapes. All sizes.

All the colors of the rainbow.

All locked onto the fence in such tight clusters that they

formed a vibrant, flower-like mural of multihued metal around the perimeter of the lake. It was curious and breathtaking.[2]

Turns out, the Russians call them "love locks," and Thom, being an expert photographer, just had to take a picture of them. The image Thom captured is worthy of an art gallery, so you can imagine how special it was when he and Joani had it framed and then gave it as a gift to my son and daughter-in-law on their wedding day. Their gift came with this note:

> In Russia, they have a custom . . .
>
> When a young bride and groom are newly married, they often take a lock, engrave their names on it, and fasten it to a fence. Then they throw the key away—into a lake, or under a bridge or out of a fast-moving car, or anyplace where it'll never be found again. Their unopenable padlock then becomes a permanent symbol of everlasting love between the new husband and new wife—a "love lock" for all the world to see.

Seriously—how cool is that?

Of course, the Russians aren't the only ones to incorporate creative symbols of love into their wedding customs. In Africa, some couples have their wrists tied together with a cloth or braided grass as they speak their wedding vows. That knotted connection symbolizes the permanence of their love for each other. In Ireland, the celtic knot is often used as part of wedding decorations. This design features "continuous, unending lines that intertwine," also as testimony of the unity and eternality of the bride and groom's love for each other. Native Americans often use a "blanket ceremony" to symbolize their commitment to each other. In this ritual, the bride and groom each discard individual blue blankets in order to be wrapped together in a new, white blanket. The white blanket is kept in the home afterward, a constant reminder of the couple's unifying love.[3]

Locks on a fence, a knot, a white blanket, every one of these symbols is memorable and beautiful in its own unique way, but there is one great symbol of love that far exceeds them all. It's an ugly thing, a brutal tool stained by blood, and it's the most beautiful emblem of love in all history. The cross.

More specifically, the cross upon which Jesus died.

I've heard those outside of Christianity scorn this symbol. "It was an instrument of torture," they say, "a cruel device used for execution. Why would anyone cling to that as a symbol of love?"

I understand their logic, but they misunderstand God's love. Just as Jesus' birth changed forever the meaning and place of the lowly manger, Jesus' death changed forever the meaning and purpose of the cross.

Before Jesus touched it, the cross was solely an instrument of execution. It was a vicious tool of oppression used by the ancient Persians, by Alexander the Great, and by the Roman Empire. And then the Son of God hung on one, and it was transformed into an eternal image of God's relentless, all-powerful love for humanity. "The cross is the revelation of God's power and wisdom," one theologian declares. "It dramatically signifies an all-encompassing reconciliation: it bridges the gap between humanity and God (Colossians 2:14); it breaks the barrier between Jew and Gentile (Ephesians 2:16); and it restores the entire cosmos (Colossians 1:20)."[4]

I want to look more closely at what the symbol of the cross really means, in practical terms, for you and me. But I have to tell you, I can't bring myself to describe the historical detail of the cross for you today. It hurts me too much emotionally to go into that place too deeply. So I will tell you this instead: read the real history of Christ and his death in John 19. That's where my gaze will linger as I write the pages that follow. And I'll share with you here the brief, brutal words that John used to describe the murder of God: "Carrying his own cross, he went out to the place of the Skull (which in Aramaic is called Golgotha). There they crucified him" (John 19:17–18).

He did not have to go, you know.

He did not have to love us to death.

Scripture reveals that Jesus' followers were willing to fight his arrest, and that he himself had access to seventy-two thousand warrior angels to fight in his defense![5] Jesus also declared, "I lay down my life. . . . No one takes it from me, but I lay it down of my own accord" (John 10:17–18). Christ went willingly to the cross, and after torture, after humiliation, after six hours of waiting to die, suspended between heaven and earth in front of a mocking crowd, "Jesus said, 'It is finished.' With that, he bowed his head and gave up his spirit" (John 19:30).

And from that moment on, the cross has never been the same. The world has never been the same. You and I have never been the same.

It is finished.

What does it mean that Jesus completed his work by dying on the cross?

It is finished.

What does it mean that he would not allow anything or anyone—not even the devil himself—to keep him from taking our place in judgment for sin?

It is finished!

What does it mean that Jesus loves us that much?

There's not enough paper or digital memory space in the world to contain all the books that could be written in answer to that last question, but maybe Guy Fleegman can help.

The Cross Means I Am No Longer Crewman #6

Guy Fleegman is one of my favorite people in the universe, even though he doesn't really exist. If you've seen the space comedy film *Galaxy Quest*, you've met Guy too. If you haven't seen it, then let me introduce him to you.

The good Mr. Fleegman—portrayed hilariously by Sam Rockwell—is a D-list actor whose greatest accomplishment thus far has been a brief cameo on the long-canceled, *Star Trek*–style sci-fi series *Galaxy Quest*. Guy's crowning role was that of Crewman #6, in episode 81.

"I got killed by a lava monster before the first commercial," Guy recalls proudly. A lovable loser, he still lives with his mom, still strikes out with the girls, and is still excited to occasionally hang out with real celebrities—like the regular cast of the *Galaxy Quest* TV show.

Well, as fate and funny scriptwriters would have it, Guy is unexpectedly swept away on a real sci-fi adventure with the *Galaxy Quest* cast—excuse me, *spaceship crew*—and soon finds himself facing one life-threatening danger after another. As the situation goes from bad to worse, every near miss makes Guy become more and more panicked and paranoid.

"I'm not even supposed to be here," he says after another near miss. "I'm just Crewman #6. I'm expendable. I'm the guy in the episode who dies to prove how serious the situation is. I've gotta get outta here!"

Finally, on a rickety shuttle ride to a nearby planet, he breaks down completely.

"I changed my mind, I want to go back," he wails. "I thought I was the crewman that stays on the ship and something is up there and it kills me. But now I'm thinking I'm the guy who gets killed by some monster five minutes after we land on the planet. I'm gonna die five minutes in . . . I'm just Crewman #6!"

For the rest of the film, Guy's entire existence is blanketed by the constant fear of his imminent demise, a consequence of the judgment of hackneyed screenwriting techniques. "I'm just a glorified extra," he says to a crew member. "I'm a dead man."

Guy Fleegman lives under a death sentence he's certain was scripted for him as Crewman #6, and the result is crippling.[6]

Now, in the *Galaxy Quest* movie, Guy's situation—and frequent emotional breakdowns—are great comedy. Some of the funniest parts of the film are when Sam Rockwell simply loses it in fear of his impending death. In real life, though, there's nothing humorous about living under a death sentence, be it judicial, medical, or otherwise. And the truth is, in a very real spiritual sense, we are all Guy Fleegmans—we are all living under the curse of a death sentence imposed by virtue of the sin that so easily rules our lives. As Proverbs 10:16 observes, "The earnings of the wicked are sin and death."

"Sin entered the world through one man [Adam]," the apostle Paul explained in his letter to the Romans, "and death through sin, and in this way death came to all people, because all sinned" (5:12). And in case we didn't get it, he emphasized it in sound-bite format just a bit later, saying, "The wages of sin is death" (Romans 6:23). Then, in a wail worthy of Guy Fleegman himself, the apostle even admitted that he, too, like all of us, lived under the judgment of sin: "Oh, what a miserable person I am! Who will free me from this life that is dominated by sin and death?" (Romans 7:24 NLT).

Sin kills the soul.

Let's not misunderstand; this sin/death economy carries with it a measure of judicial punishment. In the court of eternity, the guilt of sin warrants the death penalty. That's irrevocably true. But we must also understand that this legal aspect of sin is not the only facet of its makeup.

Yes, the punishment for sin is judicial. But that death penalty is also, in some mysterious way, elemental to the spiritual realm. That statement may seem unclear to you right now, but stick with me and it'll make more sense.

Eat fruit from the forbidden tree, God warned the first humans, and "when you eat of it you will surely die" (Genesis 2:17). This is a statement of consequence, a judgment of nature in the realm of the soul. As Benjamin Franklin put it, "Sin is not hurtful because it is forbidden, but it is forbidden because it is hurtful."[7]

Understand this: the law of sin and death is not simply heavenly legislation. It's not an arbitrary penalty akin to a hundred-dollar fine for a traffic ticket or five years of prison for theft. It's natural law of the supernatural soul, akin to gravity or the second law of thermodynamics.

Some laws exist because we say so—for example, speed limits. Other laws exist regardless of what we say—for example, gravity. The death penalty of sin is the second kind of law. It's an inescapable aspect of the way your soul was created and intended to be nurtured. Sin was never supposed to be part of the soul's equation—because sin causes death.

Here's how theologian Michael Horton explains it: "Death is not an arbitrary punishment that God deems suitable for making a point, but the legal sanction that God incorporated into the covenant of creation. God clearly announced this penalty in the beginning."[8]

Or, look at it this way: fire burns.

That's both its punishment and its inherent nature. Whether you personally feel the heat of the flame or not, fire burns. And if you get too close, fire burns *you*.

Likewise, sin kills.

That's both its punishment and its inherent nature. Whether you personally experience sin or not, sin kills. And if you and I get too close—which we have—sin kills us. Period.

Sin, by its very nature, had you marked for death—a penalty that "proves how serious the situation is." But then, Christ stepped into your role as Crewman #6! He took your death sentence upon himself. He stepped between you and the fire that burns, taking its heat in order to keep you safe and saved from it. On that brutal, bloody cross, Christ suffered your death so that his love would be your life, and mine.

It is finished.

And guess what? You and I are no longer Crewman #6. Our souls are no longer destined to live under the sentence of death. Jesus took that penalty on himself—and he eliminated it once and for all, forevermore. Isaiah prophesied of Christ:

> But he was pierced for our transgressions,
> he was crushed for our iniquities;

the punishment that brought us peace was on him,
and by his wounds we are healed.
We all, like sheep, have gone astray,
each of us has turned to our own way;
and the LORD has laid on him
the iniquity of us all. (Isaiah 53:5–6)

It is finished! God's great love saw to that. "God made him who had no sin [Jesus] to be sin for us," the apostle Paul declared, "so that in him we might become the righteousness of God" (2 Corinthians 5:21). "God demonstrates his own love for us in this: While we were still sinners, Christ died for us" (Romans 5:8).

How's that for good news? Is it any wonder that this cross of Christ has earned its place as the highest symbol of love in history? And believe it or not, there's even more good news:

The Cross Means I Am No Longer Roommate to a Tiger

I read recently about a man named Joe Taft, founder of the Exotic Feline Rescue Center in Indiana. Apparently, in states where it's not illegal, it's relatively inexpensive to buy and keep a baby lion or tiger—generally comparable to the price of a fine pedigree dog. Tiger cubs are incredibly cute and fun, except that in the space of just a year or two they become adult tigers weighing several hundred pounds and capable of ripping to shreds—and eating— their owners. What's more, tigers are notoriously untamable, fickle beasts, playful one moment and deadly the next, making no distinction between human friends and human enemies.

When casual big-cat owners realize they can't control their now-adult tigers, they call Joe Taft. His sanctuary for abandoned wild animals is the second largest in the nation and provides a habitat where lions and tigers and such can live out their days peacefully. Although Joe and his team try to avoid letting the big cats reproduce, sometimes, well, accidents happen. Cats will be cats, I guess. When there's a new cub born on the grounds at EFRC, it's hand-raised by humans until it is ready to live in the wild.

In 2002, Joe was raising one of these cubs in his own home. It was a boisterous, wild thing, growing bigger and bigger every day. Still, Joe was fully capable of controlling his tiger . . . until the man had a heart attack and subsequently underwent quintuple bypass surgery. As you can guess, having a tiger for a roommate—even a young one—was quite dangerous for a cardiac patient. Suddenly, Joe's own home became a very real threat to the weakened and recovering man. There was only one thing to do: Joe had a steel fence built around his couch.

And Joe Taft spent the bulk of his recovery time caged in his living room, eyeing his things from behind bars while the tiger roamed freely through the rest of the house, pacing and roaring and keeping Joe a literal prisoner in his own home.[9]

Now, metaphorically speaking, guess which character in that story is you and which is the tiger. Sin is like a tiger, prowling 'round your life as if it owns you, threatening your very existence with its mere presence, staring at you through the cage that imprisons you—a cage of your own making. And you're the man on the couch, seeing freedom beyond the wire but too weak to master sin by yourself, too wounded to take control of your own life and live outside the walls that hem you in spiritually, emotionally, and physically.

Here's how the apostle Paul describes that kind of life spent in captivity to sin. "The trouble is with me, for I am all too human, a slave to sin. . . . I want to do what is right, but I can't. I want to do what is good, but I don't. I don't want to do what is wrong, but I do it anyway" (Romans 7:14, 18–19 NLT).

Yeah, that pretty much describes me too. But the good news is that by virtue of his death on the cross, Christ forcibly intruded into that abusive relationship. He did more than simply tame the tiger; Jesus kicked its haunches all the way to hell. Because of Christ's love and sacrifice, I am no longer forced to be roommates with sin. Yes, sin still roars and prowls and sometimes scares me into submission, but its real power is gone, overcome completely by the love of Jesus for me.

Listen to the rest of what Paul says about that: "Who will free me from this life that is dominated by sin and death? Thank God! *The answer is in Jesus Christ our Lord*" (Romans 7:24–25 NLT, emphasis added). And listen to what Jesus himself said about it: "If the Son sets you free, you are truly free" (John 8:36 NLT). Do you hear it? Do the trumpets sound and the heralds sing to your soul in those words? Sin had made you its conquest, but then Jesus broke himself upon the cross for you. Because of that unyielding love, you are set free!

Breathe in that truth for a moment. Let it fill your senses.

You are set free! No longer are you prisoner to the threats of sin; no longer are you roommate to a tiger. Christ delivered you from captivity in a spiritual sense that is more real than your physical body. His love has liberated your soul, your life, your entirety of being.

Ancient Greeks had a unique custom to signify new freedom for former slaves. The slave and his master would travel to a temple where the master would formally "sell" his slave into the possession of the chosen god. Money would change hands—ending up in the temple treasury—and paperwork would be drawn up announcing this phrase over the slave: "For Freedom." Historians tell us that from that moment on no one could enslave the emancipated man again, because "he was the property of the god."[10]

The interesting thing about this custom for Christians is that it was this Greek phrase, "For Freedom," that Paul used to describe to Galatians our ongoing experience with Christ: "It is *for freedom* that Christ has set us free" (Galatians 5:1, emphasis added).

This freedom from the power of sin—this eternal emancipation of your soul—is no light thing. It's not a casual occurrence or an irrelevant experience. God himself has purchased you out of slavery, redeemed you with his own blood, rescued you now and for eternity. He has proclaimed that no one else can own you.

It's said that freedom is made up of two things: "freedom from" and "freedom to," and I believe it's true. In Christ, you are free from the power of sin, freed from the penalty sin requires. And in Christ, you are free to pursue intimacy with God, free to love rightly, to serve greatly, to chase after your Savior like a child finally being reunited with family.

And, because I've promised to always be honest with you, I feel obligated to tell you something important about this glorious new freedom Christ delivered to you:

The Cross Means I Am No Longer Safe

The enemies of God are not happy about the freedom Christ created for you. Like wicked slave masters, they want nothing more than to see you returned to your former state, to demand that you once again fall under the power of the penalty and influence of sin. What this means is hard, but true: you are targeted for hostility. Spiritual and physical forces alike will seek to treat you like they treated Jesus, to mock you, to condemn you, to discourage and abuse you. This is simply the way of life, especially for a Christian.

I find it funny—in a heartbreakingly tragic way—whenever I hear some new preacher or teacher telling me that freedom in Christ means only a life of health and wealth and sunshine and puppies. That I'm the child of a king, and therefore am promised only prosperity and constant escape from all hardship. Have these teachers never read the Scriptures? I wonder. Have they not listened to the promises of Jesus? Have they rewritten or simply ignored the testimony of history?

Here's what happened to Jesus' original disciples—minus Judas the betrayer, who killed himself[11]:

Andrew: Crucified on an X-shaped cross

Bartholomew: Flayed alive with knives until he died

James (son of Alphaeus): Sawed to pieces

James (son of Zebedee): Beheaded

John: Poisoned—but miraculously survived; boiled in oil—but miraculously survived; imprisoned, in his old age, on the island of Patmos, where "men worked chained to their slave barrows" in the marble mines

Matthew (Levi): Died a martyr while preaching in Ethiopia

Peter: Crucified upside down

Philip: Hanged to death

Simon (the Zealot): Sawed in half
Thaddaeus (Jude): Martyred while preaching in Persia
Thomas: Speared to death

Eleven disciples, ten brutal executions, and one subjected to awful tortures intended to kill him. Not quite what our happy-happy preachers tell us about the Christian life today, is it? I'm grateful that here in America we will not likely face the severity of hostility that Jesus' original disciples did, but we can count on the fact that this Christianity of ours will not be safe or often rewarded by this world in which we live.

I have in my possession a number of Bible promise books, and I find them very encouraging at times. I love to be reminded of God's love and grace and comfort constantly at work in my life, and these little books certainly help in that regard. But they tell only part of the story. They inevitably omit the hard but equally true promises made to me about this Christian life, such as these:

- "In this world you will have trouble" (John 16:33).
- "They will seize you and persecute you. They will hand you over to synagogues and put you in prison . . . all on account of my name" (Luke 21:12).
- "You will be handed over to be persecuted and put to death, and you will be hated by all nations because of me" (Matthew 24:9).
- "Everyone who wants to live a godly life in Christ Jesus will be persecuted" (2 Timothy 3:12).

I've sometimes toyed with the idea of writing a book about these "secret promises of God"—the unpopular pledges of pain that Scripture makes to us. Of course, I'll never write that book because no one would read it, let alone buy it! Those promises of God are too depressing, too frightening, too honest, too real. American Christians today—myself included—most often prefer happy fictions to real life. But, of course, we're not alone in that regard.

At any rate, rest assured that, as a Christian, you are promised trouble in this life—and it will come. It'll come in so many creatively redundant ways that your head will swim, your heart will cry out, and you may even become sincerely angry with God himself. That's okay because that trouble is not what defines your life; it's simply part of the pathway to glory.

Freedom always has its risks, and your pain will sometimes try to convince you that the price of your freedom in Christ is too high. When those moments inevitably come, remember Truman Burbank, and determine to match his resolve.

In case you don't know Truman, he's the title character in the movie *The Truman Show*. In this film, our hero—portrayed with wonderful humanity by Jim Carrey—is a man who has lived every moment of his life as the unwitting star of his own reality TV show. He was born on camera and has grown into adulthood in the environs of Seahaven, a city-sized soundstage where— unknown to him—hidden cameras capture his every intimate moment.

Actors have spent years playing his parents, his friends, even his wife. But the most powerful person in Truman's life is the man he can't see: Christof, the godlike director of *The Truman Show* who is hidden away in a control center high above the stage where Truman lives.

Over the course of the film, Truman begins to slowly realize that his whole, idyllic world is a fiction—that he's actually trapped inside an elaborate prison that manipulates even the pedestrians who walk their dogs on his home street. Slowly at first, and then with greater intensity and resolve, Truman determines to escape Seahaven, to break through to freedom on the other side of the man-made ocean that blocks his way.

Through trial and literal storms, through Christof's environmental and psychological attacks, through his own fears and insecurities, Truman battles until exhausted, half-dead, and in an epiphany of wonder, he finally reaches the edge of the sea. There he discovers that the blue-sky vista he's always seen from far away is actually just an enormous, painted scrim erected at the end of his horizon. He walks along the narrow pathway alongside the set's edge, up a long staircase, and finally reaches a door, painted right into the sky.

Just as he swings open the door to freedom, a voice rings out in the heavens above. It's Christof, echoing in godlike glory across Truman's universe, words resonating through a loudspeaker high over the stage.

"Truman!" Christof calls.

Startled, the prisoner turns to face the sky. He listens as his captivating "god" warns of the dangers of freedom and calls for him to stay in gilded Seahaven instead.

"Listen to me, Truman," Christof cajoles. "There's no more truth out there than there is in the world I created for you. Same lies, same deceit. But in *my* world, you have nothing to fear. . . . You can't leave, Truman. You belong here. With me."

There's a long moment of decision while Truman considers Christof's plea. Should he stay in the gilded prison of Seahaven and trust in the promises of his captor? Or should he step into freedom, into the darkness on the other side of the door, risking all on the great and terrible unknowns that await outside his cage?

Finally Truman speaks irrevocably to the sky.

"In case I don't see ya," he says with a grin in his signature farewell line of the movie, "good afternoon, good evening, and good night."

He bows, briefly stretches his arms out in the pose of a cross, then turns and walks forever out of the safety of Christof's prison and into the reckless, dangerous world.

Truman Burbank is no longer safe, but he is finally free.

It is finished!

Christ's great love on the cross has set you free, but like Truman Burbank, your freedom has not made you safe. Every day you risk unknowable dangers simply by stepping into the world. And, like Truman Burbank, your precious freedom is more than worth the risk.

Of course, you've got something the star of *The Truman Show* doesn't have, something that makes all the difference in the world. Here it is:

The Cross Means I Am No Longer Helpless

Similar to Truman's unusual circumstances, your Christian life will have its own unique emergencies—that's just the way it works. And the cross makes you a target for the enemies of God, so you must be ready for that as well. Your emergency kit, however, is something more powerful than you can fully imagine. The eternal love of God himself stands beside you in good times and bad, in sickness and in health, day or night and every moment in between. Not even death can part you from his company!

When Christ took your place on the cross, he locked you in his love and threw away the key. That means his power and patience in your life are guaranteed. His family on earth—imperfect though we all may be—is always nearby. And his intimate presence within your heart, mind, and soul is never unbound. "I am with you always," Jesus promised after his resurrection, "to the very end" (Matthew 28:20).

Trouble will come, yes. But you must also know that, because of the love that Jesus displayed on the cross, you will never be helpless in the face of hardship. No trouble will ever enslave you again to the power and penalty of sin in your life. No trouble will ever own you. No trouble will ever take your soul. Why? Because it is finished!

Because of the brutal love demonstrated on the cross, you are completely reconciled to God, reinstated into his family, lavished in his care. That means that because of the cross, you are never helpless and never alone, no matter what this world may throw at you.

Who shall separate us from the love of Christ? Shall trouble or hardship or persecution or famine or nakedness or danger or sword? As it is written:

"For your sake we face death all day long;
    we are considered as sheep to be slaughtered."

No, in all these things we are more than conquerors through him who loved us. For I am convinced that neither death nor life, neither angels nor demons, neither the present nor the future, nor any powers, neither height nor depth, nor anything else in all creation, will be able to separate us from the love of God that is in Christ Jesus our Lord. (Romans 8:35–39)

TEN

BLOODIED HOPE

If one had any real evidence that, indeed, Jesus did return from the dead, then that is the beginning of a dropping of a series of dominoes that takes us to all kinds of wonderful things.

—HUGH HEFNER[1]

If Christ has not been raised, your faith is futile.

—1 CORINTHIANS 15:17

By all observable standards, the ancient Greek philosopher Diogenes was a nutcase—a person Plato described as "Socrates gone mad."[2] Really, that sounds about right.

Diogenes of Sinope lived roughly from 412 BC to 321 BC, his life overlapping with that of Alexander the Great and Plato. He studied in the Socratic tradition and became a pioneer of what's known as Cynic philosophy, that is, pursuit of the "shortcut to virtue" found in an ascetic lifestyle. In this respect, Diogenes took the dog as his role model—often to absurd extremes.

Historians tell us that Diogenes shunned a traditional home and instead lived outdoors in a large round tub in Athens, Greece. And, in keeping with the shameless nature of a dog, "he performed natural acts like eating, urination, defecation, or masturbation in public."[3]

Stories of Diogenes are almost always colorful. At a feast, guests started mocking him and throwing bones at him . . . so he urinated on them. He preached that women should be communal sex property instead of being married to only one man. He urged women to exercise nude in public.[4] His advice in general to both genders was typically: "Hang yourself!" Although he didn't follow that last advice literally, he did fulfill its intent, committing suicide as an old man.[5]

Probably the most famous anecdote regarding Diogenes was when Alexander the Great came to Athens. The world conqueror heard that Diogenes was sunning himself and went to meet him. Standing in front of the "Dog," the great ruler asked if there was anything he could do for him. Diogenes responded curtly, "Stand out of my light!" Thankfully for Diogenes, the king was amused.

That kind of performance with Alexander is one of the main reasons why this crazy philosopher was—and still is—so well regarded in history.

Diogenes, says one historian, "set a standard of uncompromising philosophical independence and integrity in his relations with the powerful that no other ancient philosopher could equal."[6]

What's more, Diogenes often displayed remarkable intellectual clarity and prowess, preaching powerfully the value of a simple life, the unrelenting call for personal freedom, and the cheerful acceptance of hardship.

A quick wit, the crazy philosopher even bested—and embarrassed—Plato once. Using a raw, plucked chicken as an object lesson during a public debate, Diogenes forced that venerated thinker to backtrack and hastily revise his definition of man.

Scholar Luis Navia sums up Diogenes in this way, "The epitome of a long list of praiseworthy personal and intellectual traits and endowments: an absolute commitment to honesty, a remarkable independence of judgment, an unwavering decision to live a simple and unencumbered life, a paradigmatic devotion to self-sufficiency, an unparalleled attachment to freedom . . . and, above all, a tremendous courage to live in accord with his convictions."[7]

So yes, by most standards, Diogenes-who-lived-in-a-tub was clearly not playing with a full deck. Simultaneously, by most standards, he was a whip-smart man who originated and advocated groundbreaking moral ideas that still influence our lives in the Western world today.

Looking at this confusing, contradictory nature of Diogenes leads me to ask an obvious question: How do you know when the crazy man is speaking the truth?

That must have been a question the philosopher's contemporaries asked every time they saw him rolling his tub around town or defecating on a street corner.

Is the crazy man telling the truth?

How can you tell?

Now let's fast-forward a few hundred years, somewhere around AD 30, to a safe house hidden away in Jerusalem. Inside it are Jesus' disciples, Thomas among them. Just a few days ago their world had ended when their master and Lord, Jesus Christ, had been fast-tracked to the death penalty and brutally executed on a Roman cross.

Jesus was dead. Undeniably. They'd seen it happen. They'd heard the cries. They'd smelled the blood.

Yet now, to Thomas's amazement, his trusted friends were telling him that madness was truth: Jesus, who was dead, was now alive.

As Thomas listened to Andrew and James and the others telling him that they'd seen Jesus alive, that they'd stared at his nail-scarred hands and wounded side—right there in this safe house—he must have been thinking, *These guys are insane. Can these crazy men be telling me the truth? How can I tell?*

He listened at first, tried to reason with his grief-stricken, nutty friends, then finally he'd had enough nonsense. "Unless I see the nail marks in his hands," he said, "and put my finger where the nails were, and put my hand into his side, I will not believe" (John 20:25).

And in the background, you could almost imagine God grinning and whispering, "Fair enough."

Faith Is Found in Christ's Nail-Scarred Hands

We know about Doubting Thomas—also called Didymus—from his friend the apostle John, who wrote about him in the gospel of John. Here's what John revealed:

First, Thomas was something of a leader among the disciples, a man ready to die at Jesus' side. At the time when Lazarus passed away in Bethany, it was dangerous for Jesus and his followers to be seen anywhere near there. Everyone knew the enemies of Christ were in that area and looking for any opportunity to capture and kill him. In spite of that, when Jesus determined to go visit Lazarus's family, Thomas rallied the disciples with these words: "Let us also go [to Bethany], that we may die with him" (John 11:16). As events of the following days would prove, that call to loyal sacrifice was no idle boast. Thomas was betting his life on Jesus—and was among the first to bravely follow him into great danger.

The second moment when Thomas comes to the forefront is during the Last Supper, just hours before Jesus' arrest and execution. Jesus is comforting his disciples, telling them of heaven and the promise of his return. Thomas interrupts, almost like a confused child who doesn't want to miss the details of a good story.

"Lord," he says, "we don't know where you are going, so how can we know the way?"

Jesus responds with one of the most famous statements of his divinity and eternally unique redemptive purpose: "I am the way and the truth and the life," he says to Thomas. "No one comes to the Father except through me" (John 14:5–6).

John's third and final story of Thomas is the one for which he's most famous. It's recorded in John 20:19–31, and it begins with a scene where Thomas is not even present. It's the evening of the first day of the week, John tells us, barely a day after that first Easter Sunday. The disciples are gathered in a safe house, hiding, worried, fearful. The doors are locked—"for fear of the Jewish leaders." Suddenly, miraculously, Jesus himself appears in the room.

Amazing. Impossible. Yet happening!

John reported that one of the first things Jesus did was this: "He showed them his hands and side" (v. 20). Proof, as it were, that he was not only the Jesus they knew, but he was also the Jesus who died and was now alive again.

I really like the perspective that Dr. R. T. Kendall gives on this. "Once the Word became flesh," he says, ". . . it was submission to having a body forever and ever. That same body would be Jesus' body not only for some 33 years on earth, but throughout eternity. The nail prints in Jesus' hands will always be there."[8]

Jesus was alive—and he proved it irrevocably by showing his wounded hands and side to his disciples!

Only . . . Thomas wasn't there.

When his friends and fellow disciples later told Thomas of Jesus' back-from-the-dead appearance, it's no surprise that

Didymus found their worshipful tales hard to believe. He'd seen his Christ killed.

No, he'd seen more than that. He'd seen his Lord beaten beyond recognition. Tortured. Humiliated and scorned. Tormented to the point where Thomas probably sighed with agonizing relief when Jesus finally died, when his master was finally released from the terrible agony of his suffering on the cross.

That image would be hard to erase, no?

Yet now his friends were telling him it had all been just a temporary nightmare, that Jesus was no longer dead. Insane, wasn't it? Just crazy talk from grieving men desperate for any false hope.

Thomas was no fool, of course. He'd seen Jesus raise others from the dead. He'd read of rare occasions in the Old Testament when people had been raised. But he also knew that no one in history—no prophet nor priest nor any other godly man—had ever raised *himself* from the dead. It just didn't happen. Why would it be any different with Jesus?

Jesus was a great man, true. But Jesus was still a man, and death shows no favorites among humanity. Christ alive? Be serious. That was a pipe dream, a rainbow-washed wish, and they'd all better just face the truth. It was what Jesus would have wanted them to do, right?

I guess Thomas deserved his reputation as the doubter, but as the only one who hadn't yet seen the scars on Jesus' hands and side, I say history should cut him a little slack. I'm pretty sure that had I been in Thomas's place, the stories today would be about "Doubting Mike."

So yes, Thomas was the big bad Doubter. And then this happened:

A week later [Jesus'] disciples were in the house again, and Thomas was with them. Though the doors were locked, Jesus came and stood among them and said, "Peace be with you!" Then he said to Thomas, "Put your finger here; see my hands. Reach out your hand and put it into my side. Stop doubting and believe."

Thomas said to him, "My Lord and my God!"

Then Jesus told him, "Because you have seen me, you have believed; blessed are those who have not seen and yet have believed." (John 20:26–29)

Wow. No condemnation for Thomas. No punishment for his disbelief. No excommunication or suspension of relationship. Instead, Jesus tracked Thomas down, found him, and presented to Thomas his nail-scarred hands.

In those hands, Thomas found the fullness of his faith. "My Lord and my God!" he apparently shouted. Jesus was verifiably alive, and in his presence true faith could be grasped once and for all—in the scars on Christ's hands, in the piercing of his side, in his arms opened in love toward his very own Doubting Thomas.

We know that Christ didn't have to appear to Thomas. God wasn't obligated to convince Didymus of his resurrection. But—and this is the awesome part—he did it anyway. Jesus Christ went out of his way to find Thomas, to seek him out, to address his questions, and to offer himself as the answer. That's just cool, if you ask me.

Theologian William Sanford LaSor describes Thomas as an "honest doubter," and I love that. It strikes me as perfect. It suggests a thinking man who is willing to believe, but is as yet unconvinced. I tend to be that kind of man, so I relate to Thomas with sympathy and respect.

Thomas refused to believe the miracle of Jesus' resurrection, but he also refused to let that disbelief drive him away. When his friends started in with the crazy talk, he could have walked away. He could have moved on with his life, found a new cause and a more reasonable religious viewpoint—but he didn't. In spite of his initial disbelief, he deliberately stayed close to where Jesus supposedly appeared. He stayed near to those who were staying near to God. He placed himself in the one location where he knew God was most likely to appear. You have to admire him just a bit for that.

LaSor says, "Some doubters do not deserve to be classed with Thomas: those who are superficial or are not interested in the evidence; sophomoric persons who are proud of being skeptics and do not want to see any evidence that will force them to change their minds."[9] We've all known people like that.

For instance, I once challenged a self-described atheist to try an experiment with me and to pray for seven days these seven simple words: "Lord, show me the power of prayer." He refused to do it; he was afraid that something might happen that would change his mind about God!

That man was a dishonest doubter; Thomas at least was an honest one, willing to stay within reach of God—and Jesus reached out to comfort him in response. He came all the way from eternity to find Thomas and to say him, "Put your finger here; see my hands. Reach out your hand and put it into my side. Stop doubting and believe." And Thomas could only respond with, "My Lord and my God!"

Can you feel both the awe and the joy in that statement?

The complete trust and dedication he offered in those words? History records that Thomas never doubted again, serving as a missionary to the world until he was killed in India, speared to death while praying.[10]

How could a Doubting Thomas maintain such uncompromising resolve about Christ until the violent end of his days? Because he discovered what you and I must also learn: faith is found in Christ's presence.

One glimpse of Jesus and all questions were irrelevant. Jesus knew all the answers, so Thomas didn't have to. He could throw himself completely into Jesus' service, saying, "My Lord and my God!"

True, today we're not granted a physical appearance of Jesus, but still he's never far from us. He's always ready to answer honest doubt, always willing to impart confidence and faith that we can use to face anything and everything that would draw us away from him. Consider the experience of a modern-day Doubting Thomas, journalist and broadcaster Hugh Hewitt.

When his beloved father became very ill, Hugh's faith was shaken. Cancer eventually took the elder Hewitt, leaving Hugh to struggle through the aftermath. I'll let him tell you what happened:

> My father's extended illness rattled my faith. Here I was, serving as a pastor, proclaiming the power of God over life's challenges, praying for the sick, some of whom were miraculously healed. Meanwhile my own father was wasting away as cancer destroyed his body. Where was God in all this? Why could God answer my prayers for complete strangers, and not

for the dad whom I loved so dearly? Was God really there? Was he there, but unconcerned with my needs, or simply unloving?

During my struggle with doubt I took some of my own advice. I made time to be in places where God could find me. I spent many hours hiking by myself, calling out to God. My prayers were like the father who brought his son to Jesus: "I believe, help my unbelief!" I continued to seek the Lord, though he seemed very far away at times.

What happened? All I can say is that somehow God found me. He didn't solve my theological riddle. I still don't have fully satisfying answers to the problem of human suffering. I still don't know why God didn't heal my father, when he certainly could have. But what I know is that in my grief, God found me . . . I felt embraced by God's love. For me it was grace, amazing grace.[11]

Faith is found in Christ's presence, in the outstretched, nail-scarred hands. Hugh Hewitt discovered that to be true, and so did Thomas.

I don't know about you, but I have often struggled with questions about faith in God and his Christ. For every mountaintop experience with Jesus, there are valleys where it feels as though he's deliberately avoiding me, or maybe even punishing me. When those dry, grief-filled, doubting times come, I've learned to let them drive me toward Jesus instead of away from him—and to stay in his presence until that's all I need to confront my fears and unbelief. Sometimes he gives me answers and sometimes he doesn't, but like Hugh Hewitt and Doubting Thomas, through it all I've discovered this important truth: my faith belongs in Jesus' nail-scarred hands.

Peace Is Found in Christ's Nail-Scarred Hands

Faith is found in Christ's presence, that's true—but that's not all. In the outstretched hands of Jesus we also find peace, true peace that endures.

My friend Timothy Paul Jones and his wife, Rayann, adopted their daughter, Hannah, when she was seven years old. By that time, she'd lived in a half-dozen homes in two different countries and with three different sets of parents. She was, of course, glad to finally be in a permanent home where she was loved and cared for, but also wary and unsettled. So Timothy started a little morning ritual with her: every day, when it was time to get up, he'd go into the child's room and wake her with a hug.

"Each morning," Timothy says, "I slipped into Hannah's room to hold her for a few moments. Each morning she awoke with a burst of confusion and fear. Then, slowly, she drew close to me and rested."

For three months father and daughter greeted the morning this way, and then one day he went to wake her, and her eyes didn't open; she didn't startle into the day. Timothy felt a wave of panic, wondering if she was okay. He reached toward her, pulling the small child close to him. To his surprise and relief, she curled up in his arms and whispered, "I love you, Daddy." Then she drifted back to sleep while he held her.

"She knew my touch so well," Timothy says, "that she had settled into my embrace without even opening her eyes to make certain it was me. She had learned to trust my hands even when she could not see my face."[12]

The peace Hannah experienced in her father's arms—that's the kind of peace that Christ brought to us through his resurrection. That's the picture of Hannah Jones resting without worry in the arms of her father. That's the picture painted by the Greek word John used for *peace* in this text: *eirēnē*—from which we get the name "Irene." It connotes not only harmonious relationships and absence of conflict but also "the sense of rest and contentment consequent thereon." Want to know something else? With the exception of 1 John, that word, *eirēnē*, appears in every single book of the New Testament, almost as if that unique blessing belongs naturally in the lives of every Christian for all time.[13]

This is the peace that Christ brings: the ability to trust and rest in his comforting presence, regardless of what circumstance we find ourselves facing.

How do I know this? Because Jesus said so himself.

Notice what happened when Christ first appeared to the disciples, when Thomas was not present. After coming back from the dead, after seeking out his followers to rejoin them in person, the first words out of his mouth to his men were, "Peace be with you!" (John 20:19).

Then, while they stood by in awestruck joy, he showed off his scars, verifying he was the man he appeared to be: God incarnate, holding power of life and death itself. And in that delirious moment, John reports, "Again Jesus said, 'Peace be with you!'" (John 20:21).

A week later Christ came back again, this time to settle matters with Thomas. Curious what his first words were to the doubting disciple? That's right: "Peace be with you!" (John 20:26).

Jesus seems like a broken record here! And peace seems to be his song.

Isaiah prophesied that Jesus would be our "Prince of Peace," and Luke documented Christ's birth as the inauguration of his "peace on earth" (Isaiah 9:6; Luke 2:14). But after his resurrection, our Prince of Peace took that one step further, bestowing his never-ending blessing of peace on the objects of his eternal love: us.

Listen to me now: peace is found in Jesus' nail-scarred hands—his resurrection has brought this blessing as a guarantee. Does that mean we will never face hardship or conflict? That we'll always be hidden from danger and turmoil? Of course not. But it does mean that, even within the resounding furies of the wildest storms of life, even in the midst of war and persecution, we can always find the peace of Christ. We can always possess that unearthly sense of rest and contentment he promises to us when we place ourselves and our future firmly in his wounded grip.

Joy Is Found in Christ's Hands

It's such a happy moment when the disciples see Jesus alive again! Listen to how John described it: "The disciples were overjoyed when they saw the Lord" (John 20:20).

What a wonderful picture!

You might think that upon seeing a deity returned to life, the devoted would be trembling in awe, or hushed to silence, or scared out of their wits at seeing what they might think is a ghost—any of a number of sober, serious responses. But the disciples were overjoyed. Seeing Jesus alive again was both a miracle of resurrection and a happy family reunion. And why shouldn't it be? Great joy is the fruit of great love, and Jesus' return from the dead delivered them both.

Besides—and this may surprise you—people actually *liked*

Jesus. They invited him to parties (Luke 5:27–32; John 2:1–11). They had him over for dinner (Luke 7:36; 19:1–6; John 12:1–3). And people came from everywhere just to hang out with him (see pretty much any of the gospel accounts). Today, many Christians are unlikable people, but Christ himself was not that way. People enjoyed being with him. It's no surprise, then, that Jesus' disciples were overjoyed to be reunited him—especially after they thought he was gone forever.

What's even more interesting is that the Greek word John used for *overjoyed* here was not *agalliao*—the more spontaneous, loud, public expression of joy (think of football fans cheering when their team scores). That's what I would have expected, but apparently that's not quite the right description of what really happened. The word John chose to use was *chairo*—a term that expresses not simply a joyful event, but more the continual state of being joyful. It literally translates "being glad."[14]

In other words, seeing Jesus alive didn't simply make his followers erupt in temporary happiness—it planted within them a continual, lasting, state of "being glad" that would stay with them for the rest of their lives. We see it reappear over and over again throughout the book of Acts and into the letters of Paul and the others.

Jesus is alive, and when people are in his resurrected presence, they experience true, everlasting joy. It happened when Christ first appeared to his disciples, and it happens today when we seek and find his presence in our lives. "Joy . . . is not merely an emotion," Bible scholars tell us, "but a *characteristic of the Christian*"—and that joy has its root in the resurrection of Jesus.[15]

What I'm talking about here is not a joy of circumstance—though that's a fun thing too—but a joy of presence. This is the kind of joy Jesus brings, the joy of his constant nearness that overrides any other insubstantial circumstance.

Recently, my wife, Amy, saw this kind of joy in person when she traveled to Costa Rica for a short-term mission trip. While there she gave Bibles and toys to children, visited churches, and generally tried to leave an impression of Jesus on the people she saw. One person, however, left that impression on her instead.

One evening the whole mission group visited the home of a woman living in a poorer area. As Amy entered the neighborhoods surrounding the woman's home, she began to feel nervous. It was, to her view, not a safe environment. Soon they arrived at the home, which was situated in a bad part of town and looked mostly like just one large room, walls barely tacked together at the edges. My wife stood in the midst of those circumstances and felt tense and worried. Then she saw the owner of the home.

The Costa Rican woman was smiling like sunshine had found her and wrapped itself around her shoulders. She beamed with joy, she was so proud to open her home to the American missionaries, so happy to have them as her guests, to share with them her love for Christ and for his people. She brought out the best for her visitors and welcomed them with such cheerfulness and Christian hospitality that Amy left both humbled and grateful.

"In my home in America," she told me afterward, "I have so much more than this woman. But in her simple home, she has so much *joy*—and she shared it with all of us!"

This kind of enduring joy doesn't simply happen. It doesn't percolate in a life as a result of temporary circumstances. It's an unearthly joy of presence found in frequent communion with the one who keeps those awful scars imprinted firmly in his hands.

Do you want joy in your life? Do you need it like water, like oxygen? Do you find it elusive, like a puppy that just won't obey? Then learn this: joy is found in the presence of Christ.

And only in the presence of our resurrected Christ will you find the true *chairo* that you need, like water, like oxygen, in both good times and bad.

All Your Hopes and Dreams Are Found in Christ's Hands

Faith is found in the nail-scarred hands. And peace. And joy. And, perhaps most of all, hope. That's the true legacy of Doubting Thomas, a constant example of the brand-new hope for life and for eternity that's embodied in the beautiful, bloodied hands of Christ. "Because you have seen me," he told Thomas, "you have believed; blessed are those who have not seen and yet have believed" (John 20:29).

Why is that a big deal? John tells us: "These are written," he said (immediately after telling the story of Thomas), "that you may believe that Jesus is the Messiah, the Son of God, and that by believing you may have life in his name" (John 20:31).

Do you understand the hope in those words?

Jesus is alive; he proved it with his nail-scarred hands and wounded side.

Jesus is alive; he verified his deity by raising himself from the dead.

Jesus is alive; and by believing in him, you and I and anyone who will, have *life* in him. Not simply existence, but *life*, both now and forevermore.

Everything—everything—you could ever want or need or desire or hope for is all found in the life-giving, scarred hands of Christ. All your hopes, all your dreams, they rest in Jesus alone. I love the way the Reverend Billy Graham tells of this:

> I sought thrills! I found them in Christ. I looked for something that would bring perfect joy! I found it in Christ. I looked for something that would bring pleasure and that would satisfy the deepest longing of my heart! I found it in Christ. And my life has never been the same.[16]

Thomas was a doubter. He had trouble believing that everything he desired could be found in a dead-and-buried Savior. And like Billy Graham, one glimpse of Jesus' nail-scarred hands changed his life forever.

"Blessed are those who have not seen and yet have believed," Jesus promised—a pledge made for all the Doubting Thomases who would come in the millennia that followed that incredible encounter. This blessing of the resurrected Christ rests securely on your life as well as mine.

Sometimes I find it hard to recognize that blessing; sometimes I worry that I don't have that blessing at all. In those times I remember Thomas's experience.

"Reach out your hand," Jesus said to him a few thousand years ago, and today I still hear echoes of Jesus' voice speaking those words to me. "Stop doubting . . . *believe* . . ."

This is the hope, the constant hope that Thomas's embarrassing story gives to me today. Everything—all my dreams, my soul's deepest desires—it's all found in Jesus. Faith to overcome fear. A friend with whom to face tomorrow. A future to claim my past. Unbroken blessing for every moment in my present. All of it, it's in Jesus.

Sometimes life feels like a death in family; other times it's like breath in the laughter of a child. Always, though, the promise of life—real *Life*—rests in his wounded hands.

Whatever it is—your doubts, your confidence, your family, your career, your victories and defeats, your hardships, your joy, your laughter, your tears, your very existence from this moment to the next—take it all to Jesus!

Let's make a pact right now, you and me. Let's determine to spend the rest of our lives in joyful, desperate, relentless pursuit of him who loved us enough to die for us. Let's seek with unyielding desire the tender hands of the one who conquered death so that we, too, might live.

This is our bloodied, beautiful hope, guaranteed by the resurrection of our Lord and delivered to us by his very hand. May that hope be a fixture that ever rules our days. And may it begin today.

AFTERWORD

H ere are the people who matter for this story:
    You.
    Me.
And of course, Jesus.

Our adventure began on the first page of this book with a little curiosity, and people possessing a desire simply to know Jesus more.

Where does our adventure end? Certainly not here, where things are just starting to get interesting. Certainly not with the last page of this book.

I thank you for joining me on this journey of discovery, for traveling the road of Christ's life in search of the underneath things. I hope the trip was as worthwhile for you as it was for me, and I hope you'll continue the journey long after you've forgotten this book.

In the end, what I think I've discovered on this trip is this: *all that matters is Jesus.*

Yes, there are questions and miracles and strange experiences and brand-new things to discover, but everything always seems to come back to one remarkable, undeniable person.

Jesus.

In him is mischievous glory. In him is mysterious grace, and frightening wonder and anything else we could ever imagine—and most everything we can't even dream of.

So, now that we are done with the pages here, I want to encourage you to do two things. First, pass this book on to someone else—a friend, a family member, a nearby librarian, a stranger at the beach. Doesn't matter, just so it gets beyond your bookshelf and into the lives of others. Second, and most important, set *your eyes always on Jesus.* Find God in every moment of your life and let his presence be your eternal joy, between the seconds and throughout the years.

God bless you, friend. Thanks for listening, and for staying with me to the end. May you always be found holding the nail-scarred hand!

Sincerely,

Mike Nappa, 2013

NOTES

Introduction: The Racehorse

1. If you're interested, you can see a high-speed projection of Eadweard Muybridge's series photographs of Occident at http://en.wikipedia .org/wiki/Eadweard_Muybridge.
2. Rebecca Solnit, *River of Shadows* (New York: Penguin, 2004), 3, 5, 78–79, 190, 200; Charles Musser, "Program Notes: Series Photography," *The Movies Begin Volume One: The Great Train Robbery and Other Primary Works,* produced by David Shepard (Kino Video, 2002), DVD.

Chapter 1: Mischievous Glory

1. Matthew Lombardi, ed., *Fodor's Italy 2007* (New York: Fodor's Travel Publications / Random House, 2007), 504.
2. Moritz Adolph Jagendorf, *The Priceless Cats* (New York: Vanguard Press, 1956), 15–24.
3. Lombardi, ed., *Fodor's Italy,* 504.
4. "Siena Cathedral," Wikipedia.org., updated February 26, 2012, http://en.wikipedia.org/wiki/Siena_Cathedral.
5. Read the historical account of Jesus' birth in Luke 2:1–20.
6. Herschel Hobbs, *The Illustrated Life of Jesus* (Nashville, TN: Holman Reference, 2000), 58.
7. Andraé Crouch, vocal performance of "Bethlehem (The World Is Gonna Hear About You)," written by Andraé Crouch, Eden Joshua, Daryl Bennett, and Jim Guttridge, 1998, on *The Gift of Christmas,* Quest Records, CD, Track 10, lyrics transcribed by the author.
8. Linda Carlson Johnson, *Mother Teresa* (Woodbridge, CT: Blackbirch Press, 1991), 5–10.

Chapter 2: Mysterious Grace

1. Read the full story of this woman's unexpected encounter with Jesus in John 4:5–42.
2. "It's a Mystery," *Shakespeare in Love*, directed by John Madden, written by Tom Stoppard and Marc Norman (Buena Vista Home Entertainment / Miramax, 1999), DVD. Transcribed by the author.
3. Ralph Gower, *The New Manners and Customs of Bible Times* (Chicago: Moody Press, 1987), 250.
4. Chip Heath and Dan Heath, *Made to Stick* (New York: Random House, 2007), 84.
5. Ibid., 84–85.
6. Ibid., 85.

Chapter 3: Criminal Kindness

1. Carole F. Chase, ed., *Madeleine L'Engle Herself* (Colorado Springs, CO: Shaw Books, 2001), 98.
2. Michael Finkel, "Uncatchable," *GQ*, May 2012, 134–139, 182–184, http://www.gq.com/news-politics/newsmakers/201205/george-wright-fugitive-capture-story.
3. Matthew's story is also recorded in Matthew 9:9–13 and Mark 2:13–17.
4. Herschel Hobbs, *The Illustrated Life of Jesus* (Nashville, TN: Holman Reference, 2000), 80–82, 200; Craig S. Keener, *The IVP Bible Background Commentary: New Testament* (Downers Grove, IL: InterVarsity Press, 1993), 69–70; *Who Was Who in the Bible* (Nashville, TN: Thomas Nelson Publishers, 1999), 259.
5. Charles R. Swindoll, *Swindoll's New Testament Insights: Insights on Luke* (Grand Rapids, MI: Zondervan, 2012), 135.
6. Lawrence Block, *Spider, Spin Me a Web* (New York: Harper, 1988), 108.
7. Walter A. Elwell, ed., *Baker Commentary on the Bible* (Grand Rapids, MI: Baker Books, 1989), 812.
8. Audrey and Don Wood, *The Napping House* (San Diego, CA: Red Wagon Books, 1984).
9. Ken Robinson with Lou Aronica, *The Element* (New York: Viking/Penguin, 2009), 1–3.

10. Brennan Manning as quoted by Charles R. Swindoll in *Swindoll's New Testament Insights: Insights on Luke* (Grand Rapids, MI: Zondervan, 2012), 136–137.
11. Martin Luther King Jr., *Strength to Love* (Minneapolis, MN: Fortress Press, 2010), 37.
12. Keener, *The IVP Bible Background Commentary*, 202.
13. Herbert Lockyer, *All the Apostles of the Bible* (Grand Rapids, MI: Zondervan, 1972), 254; *Archaeological Study Bible* (Grand Rapids, MI: Zondervan, 2005), 1556.

Chapter 4: Frightening Wonder

1. George MacDonald, *Unspoken Sermons, Series I, II, III in one Volume*, as quoted by Henry Verplough in *3000 Quotations from the Writings of George MacDonald* (Grand Rapids, MI: Fleming H. Revell, 1996), 88.
2. "Doctors Fined for Fight in Operating Room," *New York Times*, November 28, 1993, http://www.nytimes.com/1993/11/28/us/doctors-fined-for-fight-in-operating-room.html; "Fisticuffs in the O.R. Means Fines for Docs," *Mirth & Madness*, http://www.mrmd.com/mir/fisticuffs.html, accessed November 27, 2012.
3. Read the full story of this unusual event in Mark 4:35–41.
4. James Strong, STD, LLD, "New Strong's Concise Dictionary of the Words in the Greek Testament," in *The New Strong's Exhaustive Concordance of the Bible* (Nashville, TN: Thomas Nelson Publishers, 1995, 1996), 56, s.v. "mĕgas."
5. Ibid., 52, s.v. "lailaps."
6. Ibid., 81, s.v. "Sĕismŏs."
7. In case you're wondering, I'm not one who is subject to frequent dreams and visions from God. In fact, this vision of the door is the only time I've ever experienced that kind of thing. Typically, I find God leads me more through Scripture and occasional flashes of unexpected insight. Just FYI.
8. See Matthew 27:5; *Who Was Who in the Bible* (Nashville, TN: Thomas Nelson Publishers, 1999), 211.

Chapter 5: Stolen Miracles

1. John F. Walvoord and Roy B. Zuck, *The Bible Knowledge*

Commentary: New Testament (Colorado Springs, CO: Victor Books, 1983), 95.

2. Church leaders in later times would try to rectify the gospel writers' omission in regard to this woman. Since no one knew her real name, they assigned one to her: Veronica. But it was an arbitrary choice and easily overlooked. "Veronica" barely stuck; today it's mostly ignored.
3. Her story is also recorded in Matthew 9:20–22 and Luke 8:43–48.
4. Dick Van Dyke, *My Lucky Life In and Out of Show Business* (New York: Crown Archetype, 2011), 122–123.
5. Babbie Mason, vocal performance of "Shopping List," by Larry Bryant, on *Comfort and Joy*, Word Incorporated 1992, CD.
6. Craig S. Keener, *The IVP Bible Background Commentary: New Testament* (Downers Grove, IL: InterVarsity Press, 1993), 148.
7. Walvoord and Zuck, *The Bible Knowledge Commentary*, 124.
8. Clinton E. Arnold, ed., *Zondervan Illustrated Bible Backgrounds Commentary* (Grand Rapids, MI: Zondervan, 2002), 1:237.
9. Ibid.
10. David Cote, *Wicked: The Grimmerie* (New York: Hyperion, 2005), 182.
11. Arnold, ed., *Zondervan Illustrated Bible Backgrounds Commentary*, 1:237.
12. See Matthew 9:35–36; 14:14; 15:32; 20:33–34; Mark 1:40–42; Luke 7:12–15.
13. Walvoord and Zuck, *The Bible Knowledge Commentary*, 125.
14. Keener, *The IVP Bible Background Commentary*, 148–149.
15. Aesop, "The Tortoise and the Eagle," in *Aesop's Fables*, trans. George Fyler Townsend (Garden City, NY: Doubleday & Company Inc., 1968), 55–56.

Chapter 6: Tattered Faith
1. As quoted by Franklin Graham and Donna Lee Toney in *Billy Graham in Quotes* (Nashville, TN: Thomas Nelson, 2011), 135.
2. See Matthew 3:1–4 and Mark 1:1–6.
3. Clinton E. Arnold, ed., *Zondervan Illustrated Bible Backgrounds Commentary* (Grand Rapids, MI: Zondervan, 2002), 1:71.
4. Philip Matyszak, *Ancient Rome on Five Denarii a Day* (London, Thames & Hudson Ltd., 2007), 78.

5. Ibid.
6. "Sallust," Wikipedia.org., updated March 21, 2012, http://
en.wikipedia.org/wiki/Sallust.
7. Arnold, ed., *Zondervan Illustrated Bible Backgrounds Commentary*,
1:71.
8. Randall Bedwell, ed., *Brink of Destruction* (Nashville, TN:
Cumberland House, 1999), 26.
9. Ibid., 82.
10. Ibid., 86.
11. Ibid., 109.
12. Ibid., 127.
13. Ibid., 171.
14. Ibid., 188.
15. Ibid., 198
16. George A. Buttrick, "The Gospel According to St. Matthew:
Exposition" in *The Interpreter's Bible* (Nashville, TN: Abingdon
Press, 1951), 7:379.
17. John Wesley, "Matthew" in *The Classic Bible Commentary*, ed.
Owen Collins (Wheaton, IL: Crossway Books, 1999), 925.
18. See Isaiah 29:18; 35:5 (blind see); Isaiah 35:6 (lame walk); Isaiah
53:4 (lepers healed); Isaiah 29:18–19; 35:5 (deaf hear); Isaiah
26:18–19 (dead raised); Isaiah 61:1 (good news preached to poor).
19. Charles M. Schulz, *Peanuts Treasury* (New York: Metrobooks, 1968,
2000), 42.
20. Charles R. Swindoll, *Start Where You Are* (Nashville, TN: Thomas
Nelson, 1999).

Chapter 7: Beautiful Sorrow
1. "You Found Me," lyrics by Joseph King and Isaac Slade, © EMI
April Music Inc., on *The Fray*, Epic, 2009, CD.
2. Jack Jenkins, "Poll: God's Approval Rating Barely Breaks 50
Percent," *Huffington Post*, July 27, 2011, http://www.huffingtonpost
.com/2011/07/27/god-congress-approval-rating_n_911220.html.
3. One mind I admire who has recently attempted a thoughtful
exploration of suffering is Dinesh D'Souza. I highly recommend
his work *Godforsaken* (Wheaton, IL: Tyndale House, 2012). And,
of course, C. S. Lewis's book *The Problem of Pain* (New York:

HarperOne, 1940, 1996) is required reading for anyone with serious intellectual curiosity about the topic.

4. *Dan in Real Life*, directed by Peter Hedges, written by Pierce Gardner and Peter Hedges (2008; Focus Features / Touchstone Home Entertainment, 2008), DVD.

5. C. S. Lewis, *Letters to an American Lady*, ed. Clyde S. Kilby (Grand Rapids, MI: William B. Eerdmans Publishing Company, 1967), 85.

6. Charles R. Swindoll, *Swindoll's New Testament Insights: Insights on John* (Grand Rapids, MI: Zondervan, 2010), 198.

7. C. S. Lewis, *A Grief Observed* (New York: HarperSanFranciso, 1961, 1994), 11–12.

8. Ibid., 11.

9. Ibid., 19, 21–22.

10. Lewis, *Letters to an American Lady*, 89.

11. Lewis, *A Grief Observed*, 68.

12. Edgar Johnson, *Charles Dickens: His Tragedy and Triumph*, revised and abridged (New York: The Viking Press, 1952, 1977), 125–126, 128.

13. Jerome Loving, *Mark Twain: The Adventures of Samuel L. Clemens* (Berkeley, CA: University of California Press, 2010), 62.

14. Ibid., 65–66.

Chapter 8: Insulting Greatness

1. Stan Lee, *Origins of Marvel Comics* (New York: Marvel Comics, 1974, 1997), 141. This quote is from the last panel of the comic book, Amazing Fantasy #15 (published in 1962 by Marvel Comics).

2. John F. Walvoord and Roy B. Zuck, *The Bible Knowledge Commentary* (USA: Victor Books, 1983), 320.

3. Stephen M. Miller, *The Jesus of the Bible* (Uhrichsville, OH: Barbour Publishing, 2009), 319.

4. Clinton E. Arnold, ed., *Zondervan Illustrated Bible Backgrounds Commentary* (Grand Rapids, MI: Zondervan, 2002), 2:131.

5. David Potter, *The Emperors of Rome* (New York: Metro Books, 2007, 2011), 63.

6. Lawrence O. Richards, *New Testament Life and Times* (Colorado Springs, CO: Victor, 1994, 2002), 253.

7. Read the full details of Jesus' final week in Matthew 21–27. The

calendar of events used here is taken from Warren W. Wiersbe, *The Bible Exposition Commentary: New Testament* (Colorado Springs, CO: Victor, 2001), 1:344.

8. Earl D. Radmacher, Ronald B. Allen, and H. Wayne House, *Nelson's New Illustrated Bible Commentary* (Nashville, TN: Thomas Nelson, 1999), 1344.

9. Ibid.

10. William J. Bennett, ed., *The Moral Compass* (New York, NY: Simon & Schuster, 1995), 325–327.

11. Leland Ryken, James C. Wilhoit, and Tremper Longman III, *Dictionary of Biblical Imagery* (Downers Grove, IL: IVP Academic, 1998), 774.

12. Ibid.

13. Peter G. Northouse, *Leadership* (Thousand Oaks, CA: Sage Publications, 2007), 351–352.

14. "Copyright in General," US Copyright Office, July 12, 2006, accessed November 27, 2012, http://www.copyright.gov/help/faq/faq-general.html.

Chapter 9: Brutal Love

1. Axel Alonso in an interview with *FamilyFans* e-magazine, November 1, 2011.

2. If you'd like to see lots of wonderful pictures of love locks around the world, simply run an image search using the phrase "love locks."

3. "Wedding Customs," Worldly Weddings, http://www.worldlyweddings.com, accessed November 27, 2012.

4. Leland Ryken, James C. Wilhoit, and Tremper Longman III, *Dictionary of Biblical Imagery* (Downers Grove, IL: IVP Academic, 1998), 184.

5. See Luke 22:47–53 and Matthew 26:53–54. Note that a Roman legion at full strength was six thousand soldiers, so "twelve legions" of angels referenced in Matthew would amount to seventy-two thousand in number. *ESV Study Bible* (Wheaton, IL: Crossway Bibles, 2001, 2007), 1882.

6. *Galaxy Quest,* directed by Dean Parisot, written by David Howard and Robert Gordon (1999, Dreamworks Pictures, 2000), DVD.

7. As quoted by Lissa Roche in *The Christian's Treasury* (Wheaton, IL: Crossway Books, 1995), 76.

8. Michael Horton, *The Christian Faith* (Grand Rapids, MI: Zondervan, 2011), 506.

9. Chris Heath, "18 Tigers, 17 Lions, 8 Bears, 3 Cougars, 2 Wolves, 1 Baboon, 1 Macaque, and 1 Man Dead in Ohio," *GQ*, March 2012, 189. Online version at http://www.gq.com/news-politics/newsmakers/201203/terry-thompson-ohio-zoo-massacre-chris-heath-gq-february-2012, accessed November 27, 2012.

10. W. E. Vine, Merrill F. Unger, and William White Jr., *Vine's Complete Expository Dictionary* (Nashville, TN: Thomas Nelson Publishers, 1984, 1986), 255.

11. "An Outline History of the Twelve Apostles," in *New American Standard Bible: The Open Bible Edition* (Nashville, TN: 1975, 1978), 1277–1280.

Chapter 10: Bloodied Hope

1. As quoted by Lee Strobel in *The Case for the Real Jesus* (Grand Rapids, MI: Zondervan, 2007), 105.

2. H. D. Rankin, *Sophists, Socratics, and Cynics* (London: Croom Helm, 1983), 232.

3. David Mazella, *The Making of Modern Cynicism* (Charlottesville, VA: University of Virginia Press, 2007), 25, 27, 34, 40.

4. Rankin, *Sophists, Socratics, and Cynics*, 231.

5. Ibid., 234.

6. Mazella, *The Making of Modern Cynicism*, 13.

7. Luis E. Navia, *Diogenes of Sinope: The Man in the Tub* (Westport, CT: Greenwood Press, 1998), 3.

8. R. T. Kendall, *The Sermon on the Mount* (Minneapolis, MN: Chosen Books, 2011), 93.

9. William Sanford LaSor, *Great Personalities of the New Testament* (Westwood, NJ: Fleming H. Revell Company, 1961), 163–164.

10. Herbert Lockyer, *All the Apostles of the Bible* (Grand Rapids, MI: Zondervan, 1972), 260.

11. Hugh Hewitt, *Searching for God in America* (Dallas, TX: Word Publishing, 1996), xxviii.

12. Timothy Paul Jones, *Hullabaloo* (Colorado Springs, CO: LifeJourney, 2006), 156–157.
13. W. E. Vine, Merrill F. Unger, and William White Jr., *Vine's Complete Expository Dictionary* (Nashville, TN: Thomas Nelson Publishers, 1984, 1986), 464.
14. Ibid., 266; Lawrence O. Richards, *Expository Dictionary of Bible Words* (Grand Rapids, MI: Regency/Zondervan, 1985), 362.
15. Merrill C. Tenney, *The Zondervan Pictorial Encyclopedia of the Bible* (Grand Rapids, MI: Zondervan, 1975, 1976), 3:714.
16. As quoted by Franklin Graham and Donna Lee Toney in *Billy Graham in Quotes* (Nashville, TN: Thomas Nelson, 2011), 204.

Mike Nappa watches too much TV, reads too many comic books, utters too many bad words, laughs at all the wrong jokes, and often gets in trouble because he says whatever he happens to be thinking at the moment. In spite of that, people have bought more than a million copies of Mike's books. Weird, huh? He's a best-selling and award-winning author and editor of many books, ministry resources, and magazine articles. He holds a master's degree in English and a bachelor's degree in Christian Education, with an emphasis in Bible theology.

Most of all, Mike Nappa loves Jesus, and he figures that covers over a multitude of sins. Learn more at www.MikeNappa.com and at www.FamilyFans.com.